MW01294149

After Mom:

an Insightful Journey to Healing After Death

Diane Michael

© 2018 Diane Michael, all rights reserved.

No part of this book may be reproduced, stored in a retrieval system or transmitted by any means without the sole consent and written permission of the author.

First published in March 2018
Edited by Sean Donovan – www.SeanDon.com
Cover Illustration by Thomas Murray –
www.ThomasMurrayArt.com
Cover Graphic Art Design by Scott Disbennett –
www.ShokMe.com
Cover script written in Janet Michael's own handwriting.

ISBN -13: 978-1986152051
ISBN -10: 1986152057

Printed in the United States of America

Contents

To the brave women who dig deeper in search of healing to change their hearts. May you find peace along your journey and answers in times of pain.

Introduction

Has your stomach ever felt nervous for reasons you couldn't explain deep down in your gut? That's what happened to mine every time I sat down to write this book or when I thought how it's going to help me and others. When that feeling hit me I started to practice "digging deeper" and asked myself what's going on in my subconscious that is making me feel this way? I call this the universe's nudge. Some call it intuition! All I know is that I decided to follow that uncomfortable feeling and by "digging deeper" here I am. I feel I have been called to write this book so thank you and welcome to my journey! It truly has been life-changing! I hope it is also for you.

When I was 10 years old my mother was diagnosed with breast cancer at 37. At the time of writing this book I was the same age and cannot fathom what she experienced after hearing the life-changing news. I never got the opportunity to ask her. I became a motherless daughter at 19. Before I finished this book, I had not properly dealt with this extreme loss and, in doing so, was determined to, at the minimum, pivot on the path that I was currently on. The way I had been self-medicating to cope with the pain was simply not cutting it anymore. I had wasted too much time avoiding and refusing to face the truth of what her death meant and still means to my daily life. I had pushed too many people away. I was in and out of bouts with depression and I was tired of it.

I am grateful that you too want to feel better; that you're in a place that so badly needs something that this book's title resonated with you. I want you to know that I decided to write this book not only for me but for you. It is important for me to let you know that even though we don't know each other, there is a special bond between women who no longer have their mothers. I have met many and within a minute, tears are usually shed. I'm sure you can relate.

So it's very nice to meet you and thank you again for going on this journey! My name is Diane. I have been writing all my life and have started many books but never finished until now. This is a big one for me; not only because it is my first published book, but because it "checks all the boxes." I wanted to write for therapeutic reasons, to help myself heal and grow, and I desire to help others with their struggles in losing their mother. I also experienced a lifestyle change after completing this experience. I feel truly healthy, I am making myself a priority, and I have identified areas in my life that need more attention in order to properly heal, forgive and grow.

I come from a background of strong mentors and believe in the law of attraction. If you still haven't read the book, "The Secret," it definitely is time to do so! I love the book, but also enjoy the movie very much! It's one of those life guides that I go back to every year and gain more insight every time! I have invested hours upon hours of reading self-help books. I've watched and listened to motivational speakers. I've spent years in personal coaching. I don't have a degree in nor claim to be highly educated on the subject of loss. I do, however, have a strong connection to myself, am honest with who I am and have a major desire to always be a better person. That is exactly why I decided this topic was the best for me to write. To be able to share my story and practices with others on the hopes that comfort and peace can belong in another woman's life again gives me a feeling that is indescribable. I pray this journey helps you!

Each insight will discuss parts of the grieving and healing process. From personal experience along with research I will bring some painful memories to light. After each chapter I implore you to "dig deeper". This is where the magic happens. By designing each insight and respective assignment to be done before you continue reading, I believe you will truly go inward. A lot will come up. Memories will flood in. Thoughts and feelings of the past will come to light; some you may not even have known were there. This is the time to focus on processing and growth. While reading this book, please sleep as much as possible, eat as best you can and take this seriously. I recommend only moving forward with each insight after the "dig deeper" is completed and also shared. I found that after each insight I told friends about what I had experienced and it made the process so much clearer for me.

This book will not stop the painful loss you embody with the death of your mom. This book will not help Mother's Day go away. This book will however help you address the programs that have been cemented in your lives from the diagnosis and/or death of your mother. Trust the process. Do the "dig deepers". Talk with trusted friends about what is coming to the surface. Journal about your experiences. I bet you will want to read it again in the future. Remind yourself that it is important to move forward positively. Remember that "she watches over." I know my mom would want me to be the happiest person I can be, so I am going to do my part to be happy and I hope you choose the same path as the rewards on the other side are beautiful!

Throughout the book I will be writing "mom" whether that be for mine or yours. I will not be writing, "think about your mom". I will be writing, "think about mom"! I feel this is personal and you will know when I am talking about mine, others or yours.

Are you ready to go deeper? Let's begin...

Insight 1:
The Relationship

The relationship between a mother and a daughter is unique, special and unlike any other. The bond begins at creation. You're literally connected by a cord that is your lifeline. No other person will ever share the same connection with you, for the rest of your life. She carried you inside her womb the moment your story began. Before you developed enough to even be aware, you shared every second with her throughout the pregnancy. As your senses developed, you heard her laugh, you shared her meals, and even went on walks with her. She was the first person you ever knew.

Moms are not perfect and sometimes make mistakes, but I truly believe that there is an unconditional love that is gifted to us regardless of the circumstances. Some moms know how to show love better than others. Some daughters have stronger relationships with their moms than others. What kind of relationship do you have with mom? Was it built on trust and love, or did that come later in life? Did she provide you a sense of security, or make you feel alone?

Was she your biggest fan or did she show you love from a distance? Did mom make you feel special or, at times, not good enough?

_____

_____

_____

_____

I am always curious why people think "turning into their mother" is a negative thing. I am looking forward to becoming more like mine; maybe it's because I had a wonderful relationship with her. Maybe it's because I feel like she was truly an angel sent by God. Literally!

Your experience may not be the same. You may have longed for her approval. You may have resented her opinions. She may have left you when you needed her most. The only time mine did that was the day she died; so unfortunately, I cannot relate.

I can relate to not having mom around now; her not being there for my proudest moments or times of tears. I do, however, feel that you may find solace and even a sense of healing by completing the "dig deeper" exercises throughout this book. I pray that you will find forgiveness and peace. My goal is to help YOU accomplish that and, above all, heal.

Some of you may not have many memories of mom because she passed when you were too young. I lost mom when I was almost twenty, so I cannot relate with that either; however, I still feel the "dig deepers" will awaken some buried memories. Bringing them to the surface will hopefully help you remember moments that have somehow shaped your life since her death. By going inward, you may be able to find healing in ways you never thought possible. Be open to what the brain may hold dear that was somehow forgotten.

Whether you lost mom at age 5, 25, or 65, the ripple effect is life altering. Not addressing the effects it has on you can certainly turn into a paralyzing life of denial, resentment and, if you're anything like me, anger! Mothers are supposed to die before we do. It's something that we should be prepared for, but how can one know what to plan for before something happens?

Embarking on my twenties without a mother was like walking a plank blindfolded and then landing in rough waters. I had no idea what to expect. I thought I had a grasp on death and that I was prepared for hers, but I was wrong.

After mom fought cancer for ten years, she decided she was done, and so did her body. Fortunately, her decision happened first, which gave her the beautiful gift of preparation, or so I thought. We had long conversations, heirlooms were bequeathed, questions were asked, and, most importantly, to me, forgiveness was given.

As we cuddled in her hospital bed a few days before her death, she told me what she envisioned for my future. She expressed her sadness and lament of not being there to see me get married or have children. We talked about things we knew she wouldn't be able to experience and she shared her thoughts about the direction I would take in life. She told me how much she loved me. She told me I was beautiful! She expressed how proud of me she was - and she did it all without shedding a single tear! I had a huge frog in my throat, but I did my best to maintain composure like she did. In our family crying was abnormal.

I asked for forgiveness for my immature decisions of the past; to which she responded, "oh honey, I forgot about all that years ago!" You see, I was trouble in my teens. I acted out like many do, but I *really* acted out and I did it during some of the worst times of her fight. Looking back then and now, I am so regretful for my actions and behavior, and for the things I said to her in anger. But I remain forgiven, as she said.

Even though, at the time, we thought we were hearing all her wishes, we overlooked smaller things like the pear dessert recipe she made for my eighth birthday. That delicious dish was one of me and my father's favorites. Even with all of the information on the internet, we still haven't been able to find that recipe. I tell you - get the recipes you want NOW from loved ones!

We also talked in depth about my father. She asked me to take care of him. "Take care of him? What do you mean," I curiously asked?

"Honey, I don't think your dad is going to be as good as he thinks he is," she continued. Then she proceeded to explain a lot about their relationship and how she needed to rely on me to be there for him after she was gone.

My older brother was in his senior year at Penn State. After graduation he was off to Pensacola for flight school in the Navy, so she knew I would be the one closest to dad and that I would be able to be there for him. She loved my father so much! I was very blessed to witness a great love like theirs. Even though the only time I ever remembering seeing them kiss was on her deathbed. I also only remember one time that they fought. You could feel love between them in any space. I asked them both, on separate occasions, what makes their relationship so great, and they both said the same thing, "wake up every day and put the other person first."

If you think about that, it makes perfect sense. If you wake up and put your loved one's needs first and they do the same, you are actually getting everything you want while being loving and giving. Seems simple, right? Ha! So, as you can see, even though we discussed quite a bit of what we thought was important, in retrospect, I wasn't able to get everything out that I wanted to say; therefore, I had no idea how to properly prepare for life without her.

It seems like the longer mom is gone, the more I realize how much I need her in the present, how much I needed her in the past and, of course, how important having a mom is to a woman's future. Wherever you were in life when mom died, will surely change the direction of your story and your experience as you navigate the pages in these insights.

For those who lost mom before they reached double digits, there may be fewer memories and shared moments available for recollection, but the "dig deepers" may bring up little things like the smell of her perfume or the way she scratched your back at bedtime. You may remember how she would read to you or how she pronounced certain words. If you were in your teens, you may have regrets to purge. You may have been like me – a "know-it-all" who was selfish and spent more time with friends than family. You may have experienced pain while going through major developmental stages without her there to explain or be your cheerleader. If you lost mom in your twenties, you may feel robbed in that the mother-daughter bond grew into an adult friendship, and that newfound relationship was stolen too soon. That is me! What a robbery it was, just when I finally got to a place where mom was becoming my best friend - the first person I called for my successes, challenges, or when I simply needed someone to go to the grocery store with me.

She began telling me stories of her past, memories of the times she was my age. We were forming that unique bond that only those that get to experience understand. Yep, I feel robbed! For those in their thirties, there may have been important decisions that you desperately needed advice on, or just a shoulder to cry on as you matured into your authentic self. The "dig deepers" will surely help you identify areas where you felt alone, and I trust this will help you heal. I have a few friends who lost their mothers in their forties and beyond. I can honestly say that I would have had a harder time losing mom in those years than when I did, because I know, by then, we would have been thick as thieves - the best of friends! At every age, the loss of mom is tremendous. It's a loss so profound that each year that passes seems to get harder, especially when not addressed.

According to Merriam-Webster's Dictionary, the definition of heal is:

1. a: to make free from injury or disease: to make sound or whole ~ heal a wound
   b: to make well again: to restore to health ~ heal the sick
2. a: to cause (an undesirable condition) to be overcome: mend the troubles
   b: to patch up or correct (a breach or division)
3. to restore to original purity or integrity ~ healed of sin

The antonym of heal is: injure, break, harm, destroy, etc.

Have you felt broken without mom? Have relationships been destroyed because of the after effects of your loss? Are there harmful environments around you as a result? If so, please describe:

_____

_____

_____

_____

During mom's cancer battle and after until just recently I made many choices based on my injury - based on the mother daughter relationship being destroyed. I experimented with drugs at a very early age. I drank a lot. I chose the wrong men. I walked away from strainful relationships. I was acting in a state that was not displaying any signs of healing. As you read and absorb this book, please remember the word 'heal' and, conversely, remain cognizant of its opposite meaning. Then make an educated decision as to which path you will choose to head down. I pray that there comes a time when, like me, you put your foot down because enough is enough. You do have the power to live a healed life. I pray that time is now!

If you haven't felt healing yet, stay tuned. In your own time you will. As you read each insight, recreate the experiences brought up in your life. If a question strikes a nerve with you, sit on it, journal about it, stop reading and sit in it! I believe our subconscious is so powerful and that the mind gives the body feelings of discomfort when it wants us to stop and evaluate. I believe that by doing the "dig deepers" and sharing your experience with others you trust, you WILL, at the very minimum, get on the path to finally being freed from the injury this death has created in your life.

If you have precious memories that are buried and forgotten, get ready to relive them, no matter how painful they may be. Do you ever wonder why crying sometimes feels so good? It's because you're digging up pain. The body now says, "enough is enough" as it purges these emotions. Getting things out will hurt, but it will feel way better afterwards. If you want to feel closure, you will. If you want to embrace moments of the past, you will have the opportunity as they will most likely resurface. Remember to sit in these memories for as long as you need.

There is no rush to complete this book. I designed it to be read slowly and lovingly. Be aware of all the "signs" that become evident while reading these next 11 insights. I recommend journaling about what comes up. If something you read affects you and invokes a memory, highlight the words and journal about it later. Write in the margins the memories that come to light while reading. Consider meditating on them to go even further.

The time is now if you're ready to heal. Let's begin...shall we?

DIG DEEPER #1:

Date: _____

Where in your life does the antonym of healing appear? Please circle the words.

Antonyms of HEALING include: adverse, bad, baleful, damaging, detrimental, harmful, hurtful, ill, infectious, injurious, poisonous, toxic, unhealthful, unhealthy, unhygienic, unsanitary, unwholesome.

1. _____
   _____
2. _____
   _____
3. _____
   _____

Am I ready to truly heal and why?

_____
_____
_____
_____
_____
_____
_____

A word that resonated with me is "toxic." Boy, have I had my fair share of toxic people in my life! Mom wasn't there to listen to my stories and offer her wisdom in these cases. I believe if she had been, my choices would certainly have been different.

Another word was "unhealthy." Even though I feel I have led a balanced life of healthy and unhealthy decisions, this word strikes a chord when I read it, so I know that means I need to dig deeper to better understand.

Insight 2:
The Death Sentence

It was a beautiful day in New Jersey. I was 10 years old and enjoying playing around my grandma's house. My brother and I were there for summer vacation. Their home was on the water, which was a very nice change in comparison to our days in the Pennsylvania woods. We loved our grandma's cooking, as well as having no bedtime, playing her piano, cruising on the boats, enjoying days at the shore and spending time with family. It was always a highly anticipated trip, loaded with heaps and heaps of mint chocolate chip ice cream. The green kind.

The phone rang. "Hello," I answered. It was mom. She was crying. That was highly unusual. I wondered what happened. I asked her what was wrong, but she simply asked to speak to grandma. Back in 1990, you could easily act like you were hanging up the phone but continue eavesdropping on the conversation - so I did just that. Kids nowadays will never know how the real the struggle was! Seriously though, I had never heard mom cry that fiercely before. I had only heard her cry once, and it was nothing like this. I had to know what was going on! I wondered, who died?

"Mom, it's cancer..." that was all I remember hearing before I softly hung up the receiver and froze. I remember slowly backing away from the phone. This was my first experience with surreal feelings, and the more that I go back to that moment, the more I feel as if I'm right there backing up again. It's quite crazy how your brain can go backwards and remember details of things that you didn't know were stored.

What did I just hear? What was going on? What did she mean, she has cancer? In those days, cancer wasn't like it is today. There weren't fundraising walks, commercials, even pink ribbons; at least not in the small town that I grew up in. What I'm saying is that it was rare, rarely spoken of, and confusing, especially as a ten-year-old. As far as I knew, those words meant a death sentence. None of my friend's parents had cancer. No one I knew had cancer - no family members, no neighbors, no teachers, not even anyone on our television programs. No one, except now, mom.

She was so cute; a petite 5'2,' 93-pound brunette who laughed while shrugging her shoulders. A God-loving wife and dedicated mother, she never smoked and only drank once or twice. She didn't eat terribly, and she did not work out, but she slept a lot. She breast fed both me and my brother and, overall, she was very healthy; until she was showering one day and felt a lump. She was smart enough to take action and go to the doctor quickly. Early detection did not work in her case. She was diagnosed with stage 4 breast cancer. She was only 37 years old at the time, the same age as my father. My brother was 12 and I was 10.

I never asked her how she took the news from her doctor. Now I can't help but wonder how that day went for her, and why I was never curious enough to ask her. Was she alone? Did she cry? Did she spend prior days worrying? Did the doctor embrace her and tell her it was going to be okay? When she left the doctor's office, did she take the stairs or the elevator? Did it feel surreal? Who was the first person she called? How did she manage to drive home if she was alone? What thoughts were running through her mind? Did she ask God, "why me?" Was she angry, confused, scared or a combination of all of those emotions? There are so many unanswered questions!

Now that I'm the age she was when she was diagnosed, I simply cannot fathom hearing those three words: YOU HAVE CANCER. I cannot imagine having cancer while raising a twelve-year-old and a ten-year-old. I can't even begin to wrap my brain around how my father must have felt when learning the news; or how my grandma felt hearing that her first born had developed a disease before she did. There are so many thoughts around that diagnosis that I will unfortunately never know, because I wasn't told, nor did I ever ask. It never crossed my mind. I was selfishly thinking how those words that I heard, on that phone, affected me. Her illness became my pain from that moment forward. I was more sympathetic to myself than to the person who was actually diagnosed. Can you relate? Self-preservation maybe, but looking back, the only word that I now feel applies is 'selfish.'

If your mother was diagnosed with an illness, how did you find out? What do you remember? Did she tell you in person, or over the phone? Where were you? How old were you? Did everything go dark? What did you say? How did you react? Do you know what her day was like? Did you ever ask?

_____

_____

_____

_____

_____

_____

Recently, I was reflecting on that day and I vividly remembered what happened after I hung up the phone. No one ever told me that she had cancer! I remember seeing my brother face down in a pillow on his air mattress. Did someone tell him and not me? Remember, I only knew because I was secretly on the phone. I remember feeling tension throughout the house. I remember deciding to take a bath, even though it was in the middle of the day. I will always remember the sight in the mirror as I stood naked, about to get into the tub, when my grandma knocked on the door and asked to come in. She hugged me. I saw our reflection in the mirror as she cried. It was awkward because the water was still running, I was naked, and she was holding me tightly while crying. Looking back though, she never spoke the words "your mom has cancer."

My mom didn't ask to speak to me. My dad didn't call me. No one ever mentioned it. It was like it was a known fact, without anyone ever speaking of it. As I recently remembered this, I got very angry. Why did no one ever tell me? Why didn't mom and dad sit me down and explain to me what was happening? Was I supposed to understand, on my own, at age 10?

I felt terrible for that little girl, and those feelings made me understand that I have some anger, and maybe even a little resentment, buried within me against all the adults in my life at that time. Then I began to think about mom. SHE was the one who was diagnosed. SHE was the one who truly was confused. SHE was the one who was probably angry. SHE was the one with cancer. SHE was the one that needed comforting, not me!

If mom suffered from a disease prior to death, I encourage you to find out more about the day she was diagnosed. I believe that knowing more about how it all went down would be very interesting to weigh against your own feelings. I believe by doing that, you can recreate a healing moment for your soul. Don't be discouraged if you don't find many answers to lingering questions. I have found that more memories of that day come to light over time. I have to continually remind myself to evaluate how I felt that day and then validate those feelings as not being selfish, in spite of the fact that's what I presently feel. I was 10 and did not know any better. If you have a similar experience, remember to be kind to the little girl you once were. It's part of the healing process.

If mom didn't get diagnosed with a death sentence before she died, think of the day she passed. What was she doing on that day? What was she wearing? Who was she with? Think of that day and recreate it in your mind. Use this exercise to develop some questions that you may be seeking the answers to. There's more to come in Insight 4 on the subject of the day of her death.

_____

_____

_____

_____

_____

_____

_____

When I recently asked my father about the day mom was delivered her death sentence, this is how the conversation went down:

"Dad, what happened the day mom was diagnosed?"

"What do you mean?" he answered.

"She was showering and found a lump, right?"

He took a long breath and hesitated for a moment before responding, "She went to the doctor in July, complaining about a lump - and they said it was nothing. She went back a few days later because she was sure there was something there. To satisfy her, they sent her for a biopsy on August 1st, 1990. On August 3rd, they called her and asked for her to come in for an immediate visit. That's when they told her that she had an active cancerous tumor in her right breast. Seven more times she would find out, by phone, that she had cancer or that it was back again. August 7th of the same year, she had a surgery that removed 20% of her breast."

"So, she found out by phone? So, did she call you at work to tell you or did she wait until you got home?"

"I was at work. I was always at work when I got a call from mom. That would be the first of eight bad news calls I would receive - and they always came when I was at work."

I eagerly pressed my dad for more details, "So when you got home what did she say? Was she crying?"

He hesitated and sighed, "You don't need to know details."

I got off the phone feeling like, 'how do you know I don't need the details?' I called specifically for the details! He knew I was writing a book about this and that was the reason for my call. I also respect his desire to only tell me memories that he feels he wants to share or that he feels mom would or would not want me to know. I also think that asking him this question brought up some unwelcome feelings for him - memories of always working, and maybe even a feeling of guilt for not being by her side. I feel when we respect those involved in this process, we may get the answers we are seeking in time or maybe we won't. Some things aren't meant to be shared with you at the moments you request them. There are times when things are hidden for your own protection. As you go through the healing process, remember you aren't the only one involved. You must learn to expect that information will come to you the way it's supposed to, at the time it was meant to.

I could call upon my aunt and ask her what she remembers from mom. I could ask my brother what he remembers about that day. Each will have their own recollection. Trust your gut to seek the answers YOU need to heal. Do your best to not be concerned with others' experiences and points of view. And do your best to avoid creating stories of how people felt or how they dealt with their situations. Focus on your own.

I ask myself, 'what would I gain from now knowing what she went through that day?' If I had asked her when she was alive, it would be totally different. Then she would have shared with me what she wanted, and not what I wanted or what my father wanted me to know. Looking back on the way I felt that day remains selfish, but honoring mom by wondering what she went through and realizing that I could have asked her, makes me feel forgiven. Taking time to go back and realize it was a horrific situation for all involved, especially mom, was important to me. This was necessary in order to better understand that, yes, I was hurt and angry because no one sat me down and told me that mom had cancer or suggested it would all be okay. I was mad that I didn't know all the variables or the gravity and depth of the situation. Knowing that it wasn't all about me and focusing on the fact that it was about her, has changed the memories. This process has changed my story. That process alone will help me in future situations. The way we remember moments is usually how we felt because it's the only way we truly can. In the future, I will choose to think about the other person and not myself. In times of hardship, I will definitely do my best to remember what the other person is experiencing, and I will ask appropriate questions at the appropriate time, so I can feel at peace knowing how the other person felt, before it's too late to ever know.

The anger I felt so strongly after remembering that no one told me about the cancer has now subsided, knowing how mom must have felt. Now, being the same age she was when diagnosed, I understand her situation much better. I understand that she had to first process what she was hearing, and then she had to tell the love of her life. Maybe she didn't want to burden her kids. Maybe she didn't have answers to the questions she thought our young minds would ask. Possibly she thought that she would have a quick surgery, they would get all the cancer and she would never have to bother us with the confusion the situation created. She wouldn't have to damage our innocence. Creating stories in my mind of what she was thinking isn't helpful for me. All I know is that she did what she did for the reasons that she had, and I can only think selflessly in honoring those decisions. I love how I was able to find that anger because I didn't know it was underneath. By revisiting that day, I am able to heal a little more in this process of dealing with mom's death sentence.

DIG DEEPER #2:
HOW DID I FEEL WHEN MOM WAS DIAGNOSED?
Below is a list of words that may have described your experience when you heard of mom's diagnosis. If your mom didn't have a diagnosis, then think of when you heard that she died.
Don't think too much about this – simply circle away. If a word comes to mind that isn't listed, write it down.

Confused
Alone
Sad
Punished
Fault
Fear
Destroyed
Anger
Blank
Unphased
Scared
Shocked

_____ _____ _____ _____

_____ _____ _____ _____

Where have these words shown up in your life?

1. _____

   _____

2. _____

   _____

3. _____

   _____

My words came to me immediately - alone and scared.

- I have pushed people away the moment they hurt me.
- I have always put walls up to protect myself.
- I always have one foot out the door expecting to have the floor drop out from underneath me.
- I have felt alone and not connected with family.
- I cry a lot.

Insight 3:
Teachings from Mom

I am forever seeking internal growth. I have consciously worked at being the best woman I can be since I was 26 years old. This diligent work was spawned after meeting one of my first mentors, Mena. Sometimes I have succeeded, and other times I felt as though I failed. Can you relate?

Mena was a major catalyst for seeking out change. She introduced me to the law of attraction, enneagrams, and ways to "dig deeper" in my journey to better myself, from the inside out. Part of growth, for me, has always been to envision the type of woman that I want to be and then become her! To enable this, I write down the qualities I want to embody, be known for, and to pass along to others.

I am truly blessed that my first mentor was Janet Michael, aka mom. The foundation that she taught me was the fruits of the spirit; which unfortunately, I feel, don't get much attention these days. Galatians 5:22-23 teaches us Love,

Joy, Peace, Patience, Kindness, Goodness, Faithfulness, Gentleness and Self-control. Whew! I definitely don't embody these fabulous traits on a daily basis, or weekly, for that matter. I can tell you that mom truly practiced the fruits of the spirit. Anyone who knew her would easily describe her with all of these words. I don't think everyone who knows me would do the same at this point in my life. I am, however, striving toward getting there because I want to be more like the woman that mom was! How do I do that? If you're curious about the same thing, read on...I have some suggestions!

I tend to think that I've made great strides over the 18 years that she's been gone, but then I wonder how much better of a human being I would have been if mom were still teaching me life lessons. Would I have made the same decisions if she was still alive? Would I be further along; more successful, more loved, or President, maybe? Yeah, no! It's extremely difficult to rewind and think of those types of things, because obviously, they can't change. What's done is done. Do you ever reflect on this? Do you ever think of decisions you just know you wouldn't have made if mom were alive?

Instead of dwelling on the past and who I could have been if my loving mom had been a part of my daily life and decisions, I decided that I will honor what she taught me and do my best to continue her legacy through my actions. I want to be a person that embodies her soul, as if she was here with me physically. I want to talk to her. So I do. I had pushed her out of sight and out of mind for some time. I had no pictures of her around the house. I did not remember her daily. I avoided memories and barely asked family members about her past. I brought her back to life two days a year – the day she died and her birthday, May 10th, which, by the way, was the same date that she made her mother a mother on Mother's Day. She was highlighted in the local newspaper because she was the first baby born, on that day in 1953, in Fort Benning.

Any time a memory would surface, I would have a quick cry and move on. I have obviously been living in pain; and a state of denial, until recently, when I decided I was ready to heal. It hasn't been easy. I still cry a lot, but it's a different kind of cry - almost one of final relief! Relief that I have brought her back to life and that she can still play a major role in my life. She still is, and always will be, a main character in my story.

There are now pictures of her around my condo. I am talking about her more often. I am going back in time and fondly loving our moments together. I frequently ask her to guide me. It has been a pretty amazing experience. I have remembered moments that I never thought twice of before; the way she giggled with her shoulders, how her teeth lined up so imperfectly, and the size of her tiny hands (her ring finger was a size four). My wall is finally down, and I believe that now I can focus on keeping her legacy alive by continuing to practice what she taught me. After all, she was my very first role model!

I want her to share in my successes; and I don't care that she isn't on this earth. I know she is with me. I tell her about my day. I know she is still my biggest cheerleader – standing behind me in all that I do. She is along for the ride. When I'm driving, I act like she's sitting right next to me. Just because she's dead, doesn't mean that she has to be entirely gone from my life, as I once believed. By shutting her out for so long, I allowed her death to really make her gone. There was a time when I couldn't even remember what her voice sounded like unless I played a video from the past. I allowed her soul to die. The more that I bring her into my daily life, the more I can hear her speaking to me; therefore, I know she's with me. Sometimes I can actually hear her! I feel like I have somebody in my corner again. Just because she's not with me physically, doesn't mean that she's not spiritually.

I encourage you to think about doing this: ask for parenting advice. Journal to her, telling her what the kids did and ask for guidance on how to handle it as a mother. Question her about those difficult ladies in your life. Tell her about your successes and ask her for advice when things aren't going smoothly. Again, even though you may not actually hear her you may be able to listen to what she has to say. You want her with you during the highest of highs and the lowest of lows. She can be by your side. Try it! It works for me and I pray it works for you.

DIG DEEPER #3:
Write down 10 things mom taught you. If you get stuck like I did, make a list of the qualities that you feel are inside you – that you possess. One that popped up for me was how resilient I am. Mom was diagnosed with cancer eight times in ten years – is that the definition of

resilience or what? I know I have that quality because of her. She didn't necessarily teach it to me in words, but by her actions, I have subconsciously been resilient and appreciate her for showing me this wonderful quality. Another one that came to mind when I got stuck was forgiveness. She was the most forgiving person and I want to forgive more. I feel that with healing, comes forgiveness and I am working on this daily. I am excited to become more and more like my role model and to have her as one of my forever mentors. I know the more I keep her alive the more she will guide me on my journey!

Mom taught me...

1. _____
2. _____
3. _____
4. _____
5. _____
6. _____
7. _____
8. _____
9. _____
10. _____

Maybe mine will help you...

1. To love God, John 3:16
2. To love, honor and respect a man
3. To not worry about how I look or what others think of me – to have confidence in my own skin by only using an eyelash curler
4. To develop strong relationships with women
5. To be frugal with money, live simply – reuse those plastic bags
6. That love is real
7. The fruits of the spirit
8. Resilience
9. Forgiveness
10. Honesty
11. How to do an interview
12. To be creative
13. To be a sleeper
14. That I could do anything
15. Loyalty
16. Selflessness
17. To laugh
18. To have courage

As you can see my list kept going. That's because I wrote on a piece of paper, **"What did Mom Teach Me?..."** and I put it where I could see it for days. Every time I saw it, I thought of more things she did. I encourage you to do the same, because it's really cool to see what she taught you and to ask yourself if you truly possess these qualities on a regular basis. I believe it's a blueprint of the woman she wants you to be. It's a way for her to speak to you. It also keeps her legacy alive!

Now...write down 10 things you WISH she would have taught you. These can be emotional or completely superficial. We will review this later.

1. _____
2. _____
3. _____
4. _____
5. _____
6. _____
7. _____
8. _____
9. _____
10. _____

Insight 4:
The Denial Effect

Mom died on a Friday and the following Monday was my first day as an administrative assistant at the American Cancer Society. This was my first "big girl job" and mom had helped me prep for it during her dialysis treatments. She was so adorable. She asked me hypothetical questions and then, through role play, commented on all my answers. She was a great coach. Even while her kidneys were being cleansed, she was always a beacon of light! During all her treatments she displayed the love of God and truly made people smile wherever she went. The week before she died, mom made me promise that, regardless of what happened to her in the days ahead, I had to go to work on the following Monday. I did. In a black suit.

It was an awkward start to a new job; however, my boss welcomed me and promptly asked how mom was doing. I explained that she had died on Friday. She asked what I was doing working at such a time. Then I explained what I had promised the week prior. After nine hours of work, I drove to the funeral home for mom's viewing.

On my first day, at lunch, I picked up the phone to call mom to tell her how nice everyone was being and how excited I was. This was a habit that I loved. Every day, for years, I would call her on my lunch break to check on her and see how she was doing. The minute I clocked out, I called her to check-in. She appreciated it and I loved hearing her voice even when she didn't sound like she was having a "good day." That phone call was one of the strangest moments of my life. I stared at the receiver, realizing she wouldn't be picking up on the other end. My subconscious was in denial. For a moment, I had forgotten that mom was dead. Denial is a strong beast. It's one of the seven stages of grief. It's so powerful that it's part of the first stage – "Shock and Denial." The mind numbs itself with disbelief to avoid pain and provides emotional protection. That is one-way denial is described.

The Seven Stages of Grief are:
- Shock & Denial
- Guilt
- Bargaining & Anger
- Reflection & Depression

- The Upward Turn
- Reconstruction
- Acceptance & Hope

The fact that denial is first among the other stages is pretty powerful, isn't it? Denial popped up that Monday at lunch for me, but I believe that because I had advance warning that mom was dying, most of my denial and other stages of grief actually happened while she was alive. My denial started right after I overheard that phone call. My parents didn't help with that either. As I write this, I don't want to sound like a victim, but I do want to express my truth. And sometimes when we talk about our painful experiences, we are victims - and that's okay to admit.

Shortly after mom was diagnosed, I had a similar phone experience with my father. He called Jersey, said a brief hello, and asked to talk to my brother. Again, I eavesdropped, and heard him ask him to fly to St. Martin in mom's place since the surgeons didn't feel she should be traveling so soon after her surgery. I immediately spoke up and asked, "what about me?" He chuckled, realizing I was on the phone, too, and asked if I wanted to go. Who wouldn't want to go to St. Martin...all expenses paid by my dad? It was my first time on a plane. I remember mom traveling to Jersey to be with hers and also to take us to the airport. I was nervous as I boarded the flight with my brother. I remember looking out the plane's window and seeing mom looking back at us through the terminal window while standing next to my grandma. It was a different time, back in 1990, when family and friends were allowed to walk all the way to the plane's gate.

Again, I wonder what she must have been feeling. There she was, days after having twenty percent of her breast removed, and her children were flying for their first time to meet her husband in the Caribbean. I don't speak to my grandma, so I'm not privileged to know how the conversation went that day. Did mom think we would fly off, enjoy a nice vacation with dad, and then come home, never to know she had cancer? I do know that I was in some state of denial - and I believe my brother and father were also.

What the heck were we doing? One minute I was crying, knowing mom was just served a death sentence, and the next I was drinking virgin Piña

Coladas and swimming in the Caribbean Sea. Denial didn't end there. Our family rarely spoke of mom's illness, surgeries, treatments, or our feelings about them. In fact, I don't recall a single conversation in which the whole family talked about mom's fight. Before she was diagnosed, we would have dinner together every night and talk and talk, but after she was diagnosed, she didn't cook as much. Then we ended up moving to Florida where everything changed. Remembering these moments, I am saddened that, as a family, we didn't sit down and discuss what was going on. As a family, we weren't there for one another and began living independent lives too soon.

Denial turned my heart into fear - fear of the unknown; because I simply didn't know any better. I wasn't told anything. I was left to wonder what this "cancer thing" was going to do to mom. I didn't realize that I had denial and fear in my soul, until recently going deeper and understanding both better. Fear is the false illusion that something appears real. Cancer was real, but fear set in because I thought cancer meant death, and that it was inevitable for mom; so, the illusion set in very young, that because my mom had cancer she was going to die before she should - and that was really scary! Especially thinking that exact thought at age 10 - and believe me when I say, I did.

I was always a writer, so the day we got the call in Jersey, after taking that bath, I wrote myself a postcard and actually mailed it to myself. I did this because I wanted to mark the date that I discovered mom was going to die. What?! No 10-year-old should think that way. When I see my friends' children who are 10, I can't believe that I was that age, so naive, so untarnished, when I went through what I did. I endured a lot of pain that I don't think a child can truly understand, nor process so young. That comes later and can be very damaging if not addressed (as I can attest).

In my teens, that fear turned into anger, and I started acting out. I began experimenting way too young. I wanted to grow up way too soon. I disobeyed. I cared less. I didn't need, nor want, a relationship with mom when I know she needed it most. As I now read letters she wrote me at that time, encouraging me to be the best version of myself and to stop escaping, I am saddened. I lost so many years with her because denial turned into fear, which graduated to anger. It makes a lot of sense to me now, but it took a long time to come to the realization that my actions and choices stemmed from her death sentence. I believe, that because the whole situation wasn't brought to light and discussed, I buried fear of the unknown and worries about losing mom. Who knows what would be different if we had a family meeting to discuss what was going on.

Because I was so young, I developed some major programming that has affected my life since then. My mentor, Mena, had me watch, "What the Bleep Do We Know." This helped me better understand how programming works in our brains. I'll give you the Cliffs Notes on this quirky film that explains the spiritual connection between quantum physics and consciousness. When I allowed anger to erupt because of what I was dealing with during mom's fight, my brain recorded that program, which, in turn, told my brain to act out – to be angry. The film uses a great example of why so many people are affected by alcohol. When you have something to celebrate, you want to go out and have a drink. If you're having a bad day, sometimes you want to go out and have a drink. Both days point to drinking, so that cues the brain to signal drinking regardless of which situation is at hand. The signals are identified in this film as roads paved of concrete, and to change these "roads," aka programs, a drill had to work hard for a long time to change the brain's way of thinking. So, one can imagine how challenging change really is when you look deeper at the roots and roads that have been cemented. Ok...whew! For real though, go to the library and rent that film. It makes so much sense. Thank you, Mena. I am forever grateful for your wisdom and guidance.

What "programs" have you created because of the death of mom? What areas have you abandoned because of fear or pain of losing again? How have your relationships been affected? Can you connect the dots, in reverse, to find out where these programs began?

_____

_____

_____

_____

Let's look deeper...

DIG DEEPER #4:
Go back to Chapter 3, and under "what you wish mom WOULD have taught you," ask yourself

how you're doing in those areas since these are parts of your life that you're doing on your own, without mom's teachings. Are you excelling in those areas, or are you being held back? If you're being held back, ask yourself why and then write it below.

1. _____
   _____

2. _____
   _____

3. _____
   _____

4. _____
   _____

5. _____
   _____

6. _____
   _____

7. _____
   _____

8. _____
   _____

9. _____
   _____

10. _____
    _____

For example, one of my superficial points was cooking. Mom didn't teach me how to cook, and because of that, I have always used that as an excuse as to why I don't cook; therefore, I eat out a lot. That doesn't mean that I could not learn over the past 18 years. I'm happy to say that I have recently taken up cooking and I love it. I'm also a great baker, so take that, Betty Crocker!

Another one of my issues was learning how to deal with my dad after her death. She told me, while lying in her bed a week before she died, that I was to take care of him. I didn't ask what that meant, and I had no clue how to maneuver those waters after she passed. I wish I would have asked more questions to elicit elaboration on how she thought things should play out.

Remember, your programs can be changed. You're in control of them! The more you understand where they came from, the more you can heal them by contemplating how they've affected your life, how you've been held back, and how you choose to not let it happen anymore. It may not happen overnight, but it will happen! Have patience with yourself and be kind to your heart as you feel the emotions surface.

Insight 5:
The Blame Game

I'm writing this chapter on the eighteenth anniversary of mom's death. It's either a total coincidence or the universe's little nudge. I remember what a day that was. I woke up to the sound of my father yelling from upstairs for me to come see mom. I was up late the night before and I was groggy. I slowly got out of bed and went to brush my teeth. My dad yelled again, "Diane, when I call you I need you to come now!" I knew it was time and didn't necessarily jump to his order because of that. I looked at myself in the mirror as I rinsed my mouth out and internally said, "this is it!" Those eyes staring back at me – defeated.

I walked up two sets of stairs, then walked through their long hallway and into her bedroom. That walk could have taken an hour. I knew mom would be lying there, moments from her death. There she was, all 75 pounds. She was breathing fast and her pupils were nearly black. She wasn't speaking. Dad told me to tell her that it was okay for her to go. I held her hand and did as I was instructed. I kissed her on the forehead and walked away, giving them time alone. Mom hadn't spoken in a few days and she had told me at that time that she was, "ready to meet the Lord," so I was okay with her going at that moment.

I was standing in the kitchen with my grandma when my dad appeared on the steps about thirty minutes later and said, "it's done." We had been anticipating this moment for over a month. It had actually been over ten years for me. I was almost twenty then; and now, eighteen years later, the pain of that moment is still so fresh. As I recall now, the memories are so vivid.

People can be very interesting when someone dies, can't they? That's the very nice way of putting it, isn't it? Often, they're operating in a state of denial and living in surreal moments. The day of mom's viewing was super surreal for me. After leaving the American Cancer Society office, I walked into the funeral home to find my aunt curling mom's hair. We were the only ones in the room. I saw her from a side view, lying in that casket. I paused at this moment and noticed the tears in my aunt's eyes.

"How does she look," I asked?

"She looks beautiful," she answered.

I walked up slowly to judge for myself. Mom had joked around about making sure she didn't have chin hairs or too much makeup on. My aunt was right, she looked perfect. She was lying there in a peach sweater, her best color - she was an Amway Spring. We had gone out a few days before and picked her outfit out. That's weird; going to the mall to shop for what your mother is going to be seen in for the last time. Did you have to do this? When the sales associate asked what it was for I couldn't say. I didn't want to make her feel uncomfortable, and to say it out loud would have been hard. If you had to choose her clothes, how did you decide? Was this easy for you, or did you spend hours trying to pick out the right look?

_____
_____
_____
_____

It's moments like this that those who haven't lost their moms yet can never understand. It's also moments like this that I wish we would have been more prepared for.

The aroma of flowers was a nice distraction. She was very loved and had a secular group of friends. The amount of arrangements proved that at her viewing. I walked around, reading the cards and looking at the pictures my dad had blown up of her with family and friends. *The Little Mermaid* and *Phantom of the Opera* soundtrack was playing in the background; both were two of her favorites. My immediate family and mom all wore orchid leis that were flown in from Hawaii by her best friend. These signified that she was now in her paradise – in heaven. This was a celebration of her life.

Shortly after I arrived, my brother showed up, wearing his naval uniform. He had driven back and forth from Pennsylvania multiple times over that last month. He was in his senior year at Penn State on a ROTC scholarship, majoring in biology. It was definitely not an easy time for him, but he looked dashing. We were not close, so we didn't talk much. It's sad that I have no clue what he was going through or how he felt - and vice versa. We could have been there for each other and it certainly would have helped us both get through a very difficult and emotional time.

My father took us both aside and, as best as I can remember, said, "There will be no tears. Make everyone feel welcome. This is a celebration of mom, it's not about the cancer."

It took time for me to remember that feeling and to understand how those words would forever change me. I'm not supposed to cry? Why not? This isn't sad?

Years later, while doing an exercise in my coaching with another amazing mentor, Brenda, this memory came to me and I could clearly see how that moment greatly affected me. It became evident that I buried my feelings, stuffing them deep down and suppressing them. No one needed to see that I was in pain. I was supposed to put on a happy face. I was angry at my father for that, but I also cannot imagine how he was feeling, to say that to us at the time. Remember, he was only forty-six and was entertaining a viewing for the love of his life. I cannot even imagine! Is there someone who affected you the day of mom's funeral? How did you handle that? Was it ever discussed? Do you still hold on to any resentment?

_____

_____

I was the best little greeter; making everyone feel comfortable. As friends walked in, I grabbed them and said, "come look at her, she looks so beautiful!" Each person timidly walked towards the casket with me. I'm sure that this may have been one of the first funerals that they attended. It was my first funeral as an adult. Every grandparent of mine was still alive and present. Imagine how weird that must have been for them to see mom die so young.

The day after the viewing, my father and brother were with mom's body as she was cremated. Meanwhile, a family member went to our home and took several things that were not meant for her. And when she was confronted, she basically called me a liar, because I supposedly said she could have those items. A family feud quickly erupted, which caused several of us to not speak for years. Can you relate? Were there promises made to you that someone never followed through on?

_____

_____

_____

_____

Looking back, I feel very fortunate that the

promises made to me were broken early on. I didn't learn to rely on others before getting deeply involved where my heart would have broken even harder.

My brother was never really there for me my whole life, so he wasn't very helpful after the death. Mom's best friend promised to be there for me, and within a month, she stopped calling and writing. My friends didn't know how to handle my 'new normal' and slowly everyone disappeared. I was alone. There were so many people there at the end and immediately after, but then just crickets. Now when someone I know loses someone, I always send them cards or flowers after some time has passed, because that's when I needed it most.

As time has passed, I have been able to go backwards and replay a lot of what felt as if I was having an out of body experience. This has taken time and it has required making peace with many in order to be able to really put those painful experiences in the past. Have you made peace with those who affected you through mom's death? Is there someone that you still blame for situations - maybe someone who wronged you or took advantage of your situation? A shoulder that wasn't there to cry on? Phone calls that stopped?

Write their names here:

_____

_____

_____

_____

I had no idea how angry I was, until I went deeper. Until I released my inner "you know what!" It's amazing what comes up when you give yourself permission to be mad. My memories that surfaced clearly illustrated pain and blame. There was anger for my brother for not being the big brother I needed him to be when mom was diagnosed, and during her fight against cancer. Anger toward her best friend for lying to me, saying she would always be there for me the way my mom was for her for over forty years, and definitely after her own mom died when she was twenty-four. Was her pain so unbearable that she couldn't possibly be there for me? I promise, I'm really not that needy. It was so strange. People were strange. And strange things happen.

The more I talk to others about this, the more I feel I am not alone. I had lots of anger towards family members for not doing what they promised to mom – to be there for us and not cut our family out. She asked each of them to be there and they simply weren't. I don't know about you, but a promise is a promise, especially when we are talking about dying wishes.

Blame is an ugly trait that I decided I didn't want in my life anymore. The harbored feeling of blame towards others for not doing what I thought they should have done needed to be forgiven in order for me to move on. This in itself is selfish; not understanding their reality or situation. It doesn't make it weigh any less on my soul though.

The pen is my sword and has always made me feel better. I wrote a letter to my father. I told him how telling me not to cry that day caused me to develop a pattern and habit of burying feelings. I didn't even know I felt like that until the words started flowing onto the paper while doing homework assigned by my mentor Brenda. I wrote a letter to my aunt, questioning why she didn't do what her sister asked her to do; watch over my brother and me. I wrote a letter to my grandma, questioning her actions and letting her know how she hurt my family so soon after we lost mom. After writing these letters, I burned them, letting go of resentment, blame and anger. It worked!

I recently wrote a letter to my brother; in which I was able to see his point of view on many of the gripes I had against him. I was able to clearly see how I wanted things to be a certain way and how I wanted more love from him. I wanted him to be there for me more; to be able to help me with my emotions and let me know it was going to be okay, since no one ever did. I wanted him to be big brother! Maybe he didn't have the tools to be able to comfort his own soul and mine at the same time. Maybe he was so damaged that he wasn't able to pick up my pieces. Maybe it wasn't deep at all and he simply didn't like me and never wanted anything to do with me. If that's his path, then it is what is and I cannot blame him for that. I have forgiven him for the pain I felt that he caused me. The same goes for the others. Just because I have forgiven them, does not mean that I have welcomed them back into my life. It simply means there is forgiveness, which helps with peace and healing.

As you do this chapter's "dig deeper," remember to allow feelings to flow as you write. If you're going into a certain day like mom's funeral, do your best to see the point of view of those who you felt wronged you. See from their perspective. Imagine how they may have been struggling. You will still be able to release your pain, but possibly now through different eyes.

DIG DEEPER #5:
This one is going to take some time, so please be patient and honest with yourself.

You got this! Write a letter to someone you feel has wronged you in the story of mom's death. It could be someone that was there for you then but is no longer - or someone you trusted who you feel failed you.

If you're not much of a writer, you can always use the voice-to-text feature on your phone and it will type out into a document for you. The key here is to let the emotions and memories flow. Getting these words on paper will be impactful. I believe that memories will surface that you probably haven't thought of since they happened (and they're still affecting you). Trust me!

After printing this letter, find a peaceful place to sit in nature - this can be by the beach, in the woods, or someplace where you won't be disrupted. Close your eyes and take three deep breaths. Open your eyes, read the letter out loud, and then burn it. Do this for as many people as you can. Let your inner "you know what" out and then sit in peace, knowing that forgiveness is happening. If you feel the need to actually send the letters, that is okay too. I chose not to because I didn't want the pain to be passed along to my family. We have all suffered enough. This exercise was for my own peace – to bring the memories to the surface and to forgive those who I felt wronged me in some way.

Insight 6:
Accept Apologies

After my father came downstairs to tell us mom had passed, it was my job to help my aunt change her clothes and get her ready to be transported to the funeral home. It was terrible. It was so sad. Seeing her shell laying there limp, so young, so beautiful, and so fragile; now without a soul attached. You could genuinely feel that her soul had departed. Her body was a color I can't describe, other than to say it was a shade of grayish yellow. Her mouth was slightly open, and she was completely lifeless. That was a sight I do not want to ever experience again, but death is a reality that we will all face at some point, so I recognize that I will probably have to endure that sight again in the future.

I knew the funeral home was coming to get her. I did not want to see that. No thank you! I left, realizing within five minutes that I didn't have any gas in the tank of my car. I apparently cut this guy off while turning into the gas station, because there I was, pumping my gas, when this random fella starts screaming profanities at me while hanging out of his window. Tears poured down my face. What was happening? Was this dude seriously yelling at me for cutting him off? Doesn't he know mom just died? Doesn't he know there are people at my home right this second removing her body? Doesn't he know my world just got turned upside down? That was a hard lesson to learn; that no matter what had happened to me, the world simply moved on. The world didn't stop because mine just did. It didn't allow me a grieving period. The world didn't care what was going on in my life - and neither did this guy. Did you have a moment that made you realize that the world didn't care that mom died? When did you realize that the world continued to run as it always had?

_____

_____

_____

_____

_____

_____

I am so thankful that happened to me. I learned a very valuable lesson in that moment. I learned that we never truly know what someone else is going through, what kind of moment they just came from, what kind of family situation they're dealing with, or what their personal struggles are. That moment taught me to be careful, kind and respectful to others; and to remember that I don't know what they may have gone through earlier that day or yesterday; or what battles they may be fighting internally.

In my quest for healing, I had to remember this lesson when dealing with forgiveness to those who I felt hurt me. I had to extend forgiveness to those I blamed. Remembering to understand that everyone has a different way of dealing with trauma and a different way of healing, is important in your journey.

Take my grandma for example. At the time when I felt she was disrespecting my father and acting against our family, she was probably in indescribable pain, possibly even denial. Jay Neugeboren wrote in *An Orphan's Tale*, "A wife who loses a husband is called a widow. A husband who loses a wife is called a widower. A child who loses his parents is called an orphan. There is no word for a parent who loses a child. That's how awful the loss is." For years, I didn't consider this in my anger towards my grandma. I was so focused on what I felt she did to me, to my brother, and to my father. The disrespect she displayed to mom in her death was almost unforgivable - until I dug deeper. I had to remember that there was no way I could ever imagine what this woman was going through; how it felt to lose a child, her first born, her princess. Remembering that I had no idea what she was going through, like the guy at the gas station had no clue who he was yelling at, helped me to forgive her for the things I felt were done against me. I didn't need to hear an apology; I simply decided to accept one because I could never understand her point of view in her experience with this awful situation. Conversely, she couldn't possibly know mine, or know how her actions hurt me. I think she must have felt helpless because she wasn't able to save her own daughter. She couldn't protect her from pain, or cancer, or death.

The more I have put myself in her shoes, the more I realize that I don't need an apology for things I felt she did (or anyone else did) to me. In a way, when I stop and think clearly of what it must have been like for my grandma, the more I wish I would have been there to simply comfort her. I should have let her know that I didn't understand how she must have felt or that I couldn't comprehend the pain she was going through, as it's not a comparison to the way I felt. I wish I could have hugged her and let her cry on my shoulder. I wish I would have sat there with her and listened to all her grievances, and her mine. I wish we both would have come together, instead of pushing apart. Because my anger towards her, for not being there for me, has killed yet another relationship. I have forgiven her and if I wronged her in any way, I pray that she has extended the same forgiveness to me.

Why do we care so much more about our own feelings that we forget that someone else is in pain too? Why don't we see clearly in the moment that actually being there for each other could be the best healing ingredient needed to make peace and keep love alive? If this resonates with you, is there a way that you can grow from past pain and not allow the same mistakes to happen in the future?

I didn't take into consideration anyone else's feelings after mom died. I became an even more selfish person and I still am in many ways. I sometimes visualize how things would be different if my family had been there for each other after mom died, instead of retreating into our own corners and having a good cry, alone.

Could we have all kept mom so much more 'alive' by staying close to one another? I wonder how many more stories I would know about her if I was closer to those who knew her through her whole life. I think about how many family vacations I would have gone on and how much more I would know my relatives. Together, we could have done a better job keeping her memory alive. It's very sad that I did not embody the fruits of the spirit, but instead, chose to build resentment against family members and close friends.

For many years, I thought THEY owed me an apology. I felt as though my pain was worse than theirs. I felt like they didn't think about me. They weren't there for me. They were older than me, so they should have known what to do, right? They should have been there, right? Wrong! Their path is their path, and my journey is my journey. I accept that now. How about you? Are these situations you can relate to?

Write down some memories where promises were made and broken:

_____

_____

_____

Pondering these memories creates more questions, doesn't it? I am curious how they felt about mom's death and why I felt my feelings had any more weight than theirs. Everyone loses when a loved one dies. Trying to debate one another on who had a harder time is never healthy or productive.

And when is it too late? When is it too late to accept apologies? When is it too late to apologize? Have you heard the saying, "better late than never"? Of course, you have! Let's dig deeper...

DIG DEEPER #6:
Oftentimes, healing begins with an apology; and then an acceptance of someone saying they did something wrong and they are sorry. Sometimes, two apologies end up happening in a situation. Someone starts, which makes the other person appreciate their effort and also apologize. Does it take someone verbally saying they are sorry for you to forgive or apologize yourself?

You may think that those who came to the surface in your blame game might owe you an apology. Well, the reality is they may never give you one, so why not accept the apology without physically hearing it? Have a conversation with this person through meditation. Sit quietly and do your best to actually HEAR them. I would think that when someone apologizes, they want to explain the situation, so let them explain it. As you listen, I bet you will start seeing things clearer and from their perspective, as I did with my grandma. As a result, you'll probably start to understand differently. Does this make you less angry? Are you feeling the need to apologize for something they may have misunderstood from their vantage point? Dig deep! Go really inward here and have a conversation in which you both apologize as if it was real! And then, if you feel you want to do this in real life, make it happen. What are you waiting for?

Insight 7:
Those Damn Days

Don't you despise those days when you're down, upset, and angry; and then you realize that you don't have mom around to talk to about it? For whatever reason, do you miss her more than usual when you wake up? Do you ever dig out old pictures, with tear-filled eyes, and just weep? Are there certain days that you anxiously anticipate, like the anniversary of her death or her birthday, when you know you're going to miss her even more than other? Those are damn days!

Are you lucky enough to have videos of mom like I do? Years ago, I had all of our VHS tapes transferred to DVDs to ensure I would never lose mom's voice. Wasn't it strange when you couldn't hear hers anymore? The moment I couldn't recall her sweet sound, I searched and searched for the tapes that I knew were preserving it. Now that was a day! That was one of those damn days. I cried and cried as I watched mom grab me with excitement after I placed first in the 100-yard dash at our church's youth program, "Summer's Best Two Weeks."

She was overjoyed and was proudly pointing at me while yelling at my brother saying, "She won!!" I didn't remember that moment in time. Even though she made me feel loved, I had never felt the way that video made me feel when seeing it a decade later. She was so excited for me. She was so cute and so proud! After seeing that, I knew I had to watch that moment once a year on the anniversary of her death. I had to make that a tradition because of the way it made me feel. The feeling of such extreme pain and loss was countered by such extreme happiness and being so loved.

Do you have any special traditions on special days? Are you like me in that you pull out old cards and read, read, read until you can't see through your tears? Do you bring her to life on the day she died?

_____

_____

_____

When I was in my twenties, my girlfriends and I would go out to dinner on January 28th, the day she passed. They would let me talk about memories and they would cry with me, allowing me to break down over lots of wine. It was very therapeutic. I did the same for them on the anniversary of their loved one's death. Having some kind of tradition that invokes fond memories has helped me, even though it hurts tremendously. I highly recommend this!

I also am blessed to have a few entries in a journal that mom wrote to me while knowing she was dying. I read these pages on special days and when I need to feel her more than usual. Here is an entry I would like to share:

February 10, 1998

Dear, dear Diane,

Can you believe it's been 4 years since I last wrote? I can't. Please forgive me but be thankful I've been alive to go through these four years with you! You were almost 14 when I last wrote, and now almost 18 - a legal adult! I'm so thankful I've been able to see you grow through so many difficult things and especially to see you return to the Lord. I couldn't believe you brought me encouraging Bible verses during my last cancer battle - after the mastectomy too soon after bone marrow transplant and too soon after dear Valerie's death of the same disease. She could only fight for 2 and 1/2 Years. Anyway, I was really, really sad and angry and had a lot of my own doubts about prayer, but you were one of

God's best blessings and encouragement to me. I'm also so thankful I've seen you grow into such a physically beautiful woman. I just look at you and giggle that you could be my daughter! You're so, so beautiful inside and out! And thanks for always telling me I'm beautiful even through no hair, different hair, weight gain, weight loss and no breasts. It's really been a joy to me to that you have made peace with your dad. That you now see him for who he really is and love him. He has been the greatest husband to me, and, through all my cancers, has kept me laughing and hoping and fighting to keep living with him. And your brother, well, I see positive signs of you two really becoming good friends again. I laughed when you winked at me when he was home during Christmas vacation and said, "don't worry Mom, when I make more money than he does he'll accept me!" Who knows what the future will bring? I only hope I'll be here to see more of it! Love you!!

Mom

As you see, her loving nature pops off the page, which is a great feeling I have been able to preserve. If you don't have letters or videos or a journal, you can still bring mom back to life on the days you miss her most. Visit her favorite restaurant, cook her favorite dish; whatever you can do to feel her will be challenging, but healing; I'm sure of it. Maybe after some time you won't need those traditions. This past year was the first year I didn't go through pictures, turn on the video, and cry myself to sleep on her anniversary. For some reason, this year I was sad and felt a loss, but I didn't need to do the same rituals I had always done. By going deeper, I have experienced a huge sense of healing in which some of the ways I dealt with the loss before are no longer needed.

There are other days some people wouldn't understand, but we motherless daughters will; days like Mother's Day. I don't know about you, but I despise Mother's Day now. I used to love it. I would give my mom flowers, write her a card, and buy her things for the bath like scented crystals, foaming bubbles, and pillows. I made the day all about her, and she loved it. She was a very simple woman and rarely bought anything for herself, so on Mother's Day she gladly accepted the attention. She had a different look that day. You could tell she really enjoyed the fact that I made a fuss about her. She truly loved being a mother. It's all that she ever wanted to be; a mom and a wife. She told me several times the only reason she went to college was to meet a husband.

It's very hard for me to walk by a Hallmark store or down the card aisle at the supermarket around Mother's Day. Seeing the title alone will hit me right in my gut. It makes me feel numb. It's a moment when the world is reminding me that I don't have a mother. It's one thing when I remind myself, but it's another when the world decides to shout, "you don't have a mom!" It's quite a kick in the stomach. Do you ever feel like this?

What did you do for your mom on her birthday?

_____

_____

How did she look when you gave her your presents?

_____

_____

How did you celebrate Mother's Day with her?

_____

_____

When you see the Hallmark store or go down the aisle in the grocery store when the Mother's

Day cards are on display, do you get sad?

_____

_____

What about when you see a mother and daughter together? How does that affect you?

_____

_____

_____

_____

I get very envious, sad, and a bit angry. I will stare at a mother and daughter and watch their interactions, noticing how the mom looks at the daughter when picking out clothes or how they laugh while sitting at a restaurant. Oh, how I wish I had those moments with mom now. I wish I wasn't robbed of those feelings that many people probably take for granted.

Are there any memories of Mother's Day that aren't positive for you and do you need to revisit them in order to heal?

_____

_____

As I write this, I recall the second Mother's Day after mom died. My father had started seriously dating a woman and we were supposed to meet for dinner that night. I did not know the woman was going to join us. I wasn't given a heads up and was hurt when I saw them walk in. As they entered, I was so angry that he brought another woman to a Mother's Day dinner.

As they sat down, a hostess came around and handed this woman a rose and said, "Happy Mother's Day," and she did not correct her. In my mind, I was screaming at the top of my lungs, "She is not a mother! She is not MY mother! Take the rose back!" I'm sure my father didn't realize, that by bringing her, I would get upset; and I'm sure the woman didn't think anything of it, because if she did, why would she be there? I certainly would never want to spend a dinner with a father and daughter on Mother's Day when the mom had passed, but then again, not everyone will understand sensitivity the way I do. Have you had to deal with anything like that?

Going back to not understanding someone else's point of view, I have to think that my father may have needed her that day more than he thought I needed to be alone with him. Who knows, he may have told her that, and that is why she was there - to be there for him. The more I think about how I have been hurt, the more I realize others were hurting too. I'm reminded of *The Four Agreements*. If you haven't read this life-changing book by bestselling author, Don Miguel Ruiz, I highly encourage you to do so. This was another recommendation by one of my mentors.

The Four Agreements are:
1. Be impeccable with your word.
2. Don't take anything personally.
3. Don't make assumptions.
4. Always do your best.

Seems simple, right? So, number three comes up a lot when I rewind and dig deeper, trying to better understand my point of view, but also not create stories about what others were going through. If moments mean enough to me to understand, then I ask those involved - and every time I do, their recollection is very different from the way I remember things. This never changes how memories affected me. It reminds me, however, that creating stories and making assumptions does not serve me in any way. Creating assumptions is truly wasting time - time that I can spend enjoying this beautiful life!

I'm starting to feel a lot better on those damn days! Mother's Day always creeps up on me, but now that I am aware that my feelings of sadness and envy are real and that they are completely natural, the more I have been able to stop, pause, and be thankful for the years I did get to celebrate with mom. I am thankful for the moments and memories of the past and will do my best to keep them alive, instead of harboring feelings of loss.

DIG DEEPER #7:
Are there certain days of the year where mom's death affects you differently than others? Mother's Day? Her Anniversary? Her birthday? Your birthday? Which ones?...

_____
_____
_____
_____

Is there anyone that makes you feel worse on these days?

I have a dear friend who lost her mom on Christmas Day. She has had a very hard time being able to enjoy and celebrate every year. She also mentioned that her husband and children don't understand that she has different needs on that day and that she requires more support than usual. She has said that they simply "don't get it." If you had, or have, someone that doesn't "get it" write down who it is and how it affects you.

_____
_____
_____
_____

Is there anything you can do to change the feelings associated with both points above? Instead of being sad on Mother's Day, can you honor mom by doing something she loved? If someone hasn't been able to be there for you the way that you would have liked, are you able to explain your needs to them? Are you able to forgive them for not being able to understand? Write down some ways you may be able to change the narrative.

_____
_____
_____
_____
_____
_____

Insight 8:
Share Your Reality

You are doing a great job! You have dug deep. You have identified how you felt the day mom died. You have remembered the countless things she taught you. You have reviewed programs you created because of her death. You've written letters and hopefully forgiven those who may have not been there for you when you needed them most. You may have even heard apologies from them by digging deep and allowing yourself to be open, vulnerable, and accepting of the change that comes from doing this self-work. You are doing great! This process is far from easy. I recently explained to a friend how the "dig deepers" work, and she simply said, "I could never do that."

So, what's your current reality? Have you identified whether you're living in denial or acceptance? Are you angry and holding on to resentment?

_____

_____

Were there people who you felt wronged you, but you now understand better?

_____

_____

Are you taking the "dig deepers" seriously? Are you really doing them or just skimming through them? I encourage you to take your time and to see what naturally comes up. Again, this isn't easy. Again, this can be life-changing!

I truly hope each insight is helping you and that you share your experience with others as well. I feel like a form of healing takes place when I release words to others. Getting them on paper is one thing but being able to express my emotions through my facial expressions and body language and hearing my voice is very powerful. The more I spoke, the more people spoke back to me. People started telling me about their struggles. They started to share their stories of losing their mothers. Some told me stories about their family members or friends they lost. A few even mentioned, that because they were mothers, they wanted to do the "dig deepers" because some things may come up that will give them the opportunity to share before loss actually happens. How cool is that?

It is pretty amazing what can happen when we share our authentic feelings with others. I have been overwhelmed with the wonderful response I have received from so many people. It also made me realize that so many people experience loss, and so often the grieving process gets pushed deep down because of life or because sometimes it's just easier. I can speak from personal experience that keeping things in only hurt me more. The more time that went by, the harder it was for me to go deep. So much has happened, causing the truth to be buried. Facing these memories and painful experiences isn't easy.

Being prepared for reality is always a good thing. If I was a mother, I certainly would be having deep conversations with my kids on a regular basis about how much I love them and what I want for them. I believe I would share, share, share - because I know that the opposite is so painful. If you are a mother, I highly encourage you to do your best to communicate with your kids in a way that you know may be hard at the time, but beneficial in the future. If you would have preferred that mom had shared with you in another way, then remember to not follow in the same footsteps. It's always easiest to ignore difficult situations. It's simple to brush things under the rug, but over time, as you've probably experienced, it's not so easy. Things under the rug always turn into stumbling blocks in one way or another.

As I completed each "dig deeper," I had to take time in between to process and to heal. Going backwards may be challenging and dealing with what comes up sure isn't painless. Give yourself lots of love and credit for working on growth. I can speak from personal experience that I have become much "lighter" since dealing directly with my own heavy stuff. I have been so much happier since I started to face the reality of what I have been shutting the door on for nearly two decades.

Even in business things have shifted. Instead of getting upset about a situation, I am now able to understand that I have no control over certain circumstances; therefore, I can now just go with the flow. These "dig deepers" haven't addressed that, but my overall attitude, the way I'm dealing with situations, and the way I feel has definitely adjusted in a positive way. I feel that the buried emotions and anger underneath them created a ripple that was affecting other areas in my life. This includes how I responded to being let down or how easily I got frustrated when things didn't go my way. I believe, as we dig and get rid of the past, we become healthier in all ways. It's a powerful thing to invest internally!

Many people will run from memories of pain. The brain may also bury trauma, so sometimes you have to work hard to find your own truth, your reality - in order to heal. When it comes to facing the truths of the past, I am reminded of a ball being held under water. It will stay down as long as you hold it there, but the minute you release your grip, the ball comes exploding up to the surface. How have you been handling your emotions that have surfaced? Have you been crying? Are you sleeping better?

_____

_____

_____

_____

How have your loved ones embraced you while sharing your progress as you navigate through each insight?

_____

_____

Are you writing more in your journal? Are you healing?

_____

_____

I hope you are proud of yourself and I pray you are experiencing new emotions of memories of the past. Experienced first-hand, I know that by doing the "dig deepers" I have been able to see the past with new eyes – with a fresh perspective, without rewriting history. I trust you are being open and truthful to yourself and exploring the path of forgiveness. The more honest we are about our pain, the quicker we can move forward; the quicker we will heal.

The unfortunate reality is we will never be able to depend on mom again. That truth in itself is unimaginable to so many people. Think about how many times you have shared your story with those who still have their mom. How do they respond? Do you hear them say they could never endure that and how they can't fathom the thought?

_____

_____

When I talk about mom, I often see tear-filled eyes looking back at me. People feel very sorry for me. I hate that! I don't appreciate pity the same way I despise hearing people say they're sorry when I tell them mom has passed. I know it's a blanket, general response people have, but what are they sorry about? What did they do? I am very cautious when someone tells me someone close to them died. I can, with a great deal of certainty, say that I have never apologized for someone else's death since mom passed. I do what I notice most people do not do with me - I ask questions. And then I ask more questions. The more the better. I ask how long it's been and sometimes, how it happened. I ask what age they were when it happened and how they are doing now. I have never once felt that the person did not want to talk about their situation. In fact, not once did they not open up and start to express their story. I find that it's hard to see people's pain but knowing that I may be comforting them by simply listening, gives me good juju for the next time I tell someone about mom. And we all need more good juju in our lives, don't we?

I will always remember going out to lunch with mom when I was eighteen along with a friend's mother. Mom was talking about her cancer treatment and the other woman kept changing the subject. Mom kept going back to her stories. Again, the woman tried to switch the subject to something "lighter." I was so proud of mom because she stopped his mother from talking and said something like, "This is my world, this is my reality, and I appreciate you listening to what my days are like. Cancer is part of me and my treatments are part of my daily routine. I am not trying to make you uncomfortable. I'm trying to talk with you about my reality. I'm talking to you about me!" That was such a powerful moment. I realized that her reality was so uncomfortable for some to acknowledge, but she had embraced her journey and wanted to share it with others. She simply wanted to be heard even though it may have made people uncomfortable.

The same thing happens to me when I choose to talk about mom. Some people are one hundred percent engaged. They want to know more – they ask questions, but that is rare. I love talking about mom and respect those that like to hear about her. I feel as if they appreciate my reality and vulnerability and, even though some cannot relate, they listen. Others want to change the subject quickly and I can tell they are very uncomfortable - and that's okay too. Not everyone needs to listen. Not everyone has to be comfortable with my uncomfortable stories, but they are my stories and I will continue to tell them whether they make people uncomfortable or not.

Living your truth is very important in your healing process. If you get emotional, or shed some tears, or have to stop talking and blow your nose, that's all part of the healing journey. It's part of letting your ball surface from underneath the water. If you're not someone who likes to share your feelings with others, may I suggest that when it comes to mom, you do? If it's too hard for you, then journal, journal, journal! The words need an opportunity to get out from deep down, thus helping heal the wounds in the heart, mind and soul. Plus, by talking about mom, you keep her alive. More on that in Insight 11.

Who do you talk to when you're having a bad day? Who do you tell stories about mom to? Do you have friends who call every year on the anniversary of her death? It's important to have a special person you can confide in within your circle. Mentors are amazing too.

I am so thankful for:

_____

_____

_____

Each of my mentors has helped make my authentic journey so powerful. With their consistent support and keeping me accountable, I have been able to dive in deeper and not walk away when the going gets tough. One of my mentors taught me about my blind spots. Have you ever looked into yours? The closest people to me saw that I was struggling with the death of mom, but never said anything. They saw my blind spots. Some were so uncomfortable with me talking about mom, they would purposely not talk about theirs or they would change the subject when I did. My mentors were always there to identify what I was trying to avoid – possibly things that I didn't see. That's why I have always had a mentor, because sometimes a self-help book or friends cannot address my blind spots, causing them to get buried again.

Another mentor helped me to identify lies that I was telling myself. For instance, I would tell people how lucky I was to have had the death experience I did. My robotic response to people when I saw their eyes after hearing I lost mom was, *"You know, I'm really blessed to have had the time with my mom like I did. On her deathbed she held me, and we talked for hours about what she wanted for me in my future and I was able to ask her everything I needed to. I have no regrets. I cannot imagine losing my mom in a car accident or from a heart attack. They didn't get the opportunity, like I did, to be able to say everything they wanted to. Having that time with her...I just feel so lucky."* Some of that was true, but come on. You can clearly see that I had to go deeper to understand that what I was saying was certainly not the truth, and that I needed to stop lying to myself. Stop lying about being okay. I had to be okay with not being okay; and I had to have a desire to want to get better. I had gotten used to living in pain. I had gotten comfortable living in discomfort. Burying emotions and not dealing with my issues became easier, but over time became a huge burden that affected many areas in my life - both personally and professionally. I had to come to terms with present and past reality and choose not to be afraid of my own true feelings about everything surrounding the death of mom.

Someone once asked me how I was able to get over the death of mom. My response was, "I'll let you know, any day now." We never "get over" a death. Time truly doesn't heal all wounds. Sometimes I feel like the pain actually gets worse the longer mom is gone. She has missed so much. It takes real work to be truthful with ourselves and to identify the symptoms of the loss. Sometimes we need more help to be able to see the blind spots, and that's okay. My family was always "against" counseling and therapy. I don't know if it was the era or what, but I have gotten a ton of support through the years, both professionally and personally, through my mentors. Seek out a mentor if you don't have one. When doing so, look for someone who possess the qualities that you strive to have and become. All of mine have changed my life for the better. If you need therapy, go get it. Be proud that you want to be the healthiest version of yourself! Please keep working on you! Keep doing the "dig deepers" and commit to really processing them. Remember the old saying, after the rain, truly does come a rainbow.

"Life is a special occasion – don't miss it," Ken Blanchard wrote. Remember to live your life to its fullest. It's what mom would want!

DIG DEEPER #8:

Today, tell someone your story about mom. Explain to them how old she was when she died. Express how you felt when she passed. Talk about this book and mention the work you've been doing. Get into it. If you cry, you cry. If they look uncomfortable, sit in the discomfort. The more you are comfortable with talking about mom and your own experience, the more your sacred self will help you heal. If you just aren't someone who wants to share this trauma with others, journal as if you were talking to someone. Imagine that someone asks you about mom – how do you respond?

Remember, by sharing your experience, you may be helping someone you didn't know needed support. You may be encouraging someone else to dig deeper to find their voice and their strength to be able to talk about their mom and their grief. Your words, your truth, and your reality will always serve you - and if in the process it helps others too, then that's wonderful, isn't it?

Insight 9:
Time to Confront Mom

This was the hardest "dig deeper" for me to relive. As I begin to write, my stomach feels nervous and I feel inclined to put this off, which tells me this may be hard for you as well. Again, the universe nudges us into a moment of change and growth.

It's time to confront mom. It's time to uncover the most intimate parts of your love for her. It's time to rewind time from birth on. It's time to express to her how you've felt since she departed. It's time to tell her how much you love and miss her. It's time to uncover any missed opportunities from when she was alive. It's time to see how you really feel about her.

As I was piecing together my issues with anger during months of coaching, something shocking happened - I realized how angry I was at mom. I was really mad at her, which made me feel a bit guilty. This was very confusing. How was I upset with the one who really suffered? The woman who I looked up to, who showed me love in its most perfect form; how could I have anything against her? Let me share...

My wonderful mentor Brenda challenged me to write mom a letter. She suggested I tell her what I was missing in life because she wasn't there. The idea was to allow my feelings to flow out about the pain I had endured during her fight against cancer and after her death. I was to let mom know what life was like now without her. Easy breezy I thought, as I sat down to write.

It started with how much I missed her. Then I began writing how things have been so hard without her. I expressed how much I missed her being there for me and how much I missed our daily lunch conversations over the phone. I realized how her just being on the other end of the phone meant so much to me even though, most of the time, it was casual chit chat. The words I was writing invoked lots of tears. I wrote in great detail about my life after her death. I bragged about all my successes and told her how proud of me she would have been. She always told me she was proud of me (after my teenage years), but she really didn't get to witness anything since I was so young. I was just only beginning to excel in life when she passed.

I shared my troubles, talked about relationships, and expressed how others in the family chose to not support us after she passed; and I said how disappointed she would have been with their actions (or lack thereof). It was a very long letter and it flowed easily. Words were coming out of thin air and I could barely keep up with my writing. It was like I was having an actual conversation with her, picking up right where we left off. She was listening, and I was talking – well, writing.

After pages of flowing conversation, I went a bit deeper. I wrote about how much I loved her. I wrote how life was not the same without her in it. I thanked her for everything she taught me. I thanked her for being such a strong woman and for leading by example. I thanked her for cultivating the fruits of the spirit and I told her how much she meant to me. I wrote so many paragraphs about missing her. And then, out of nowhere, I got angry. Very angry! The tears stopped; and that's when the words really came out!

It felt as though someone else had grabbed my pen and started writing for me. It was a surreal experience and I am so grateful it happened. I asked her why. I asked her how she could leave me. I questioned what she was thinking by asking me to take care of my father. How did she expect me to do that? I told her I was angry with her and I didn't feel guilty for expressing that! There were a lot of "how could you" and even more "you left me" and yet even more "why's"! What just happened? Where did all of that come from? I had no idea how upset I was with her. Sure, I knew I was angry, but never did I make the connection that I was really angry at her! I was totally crying while writing and it was the deep down, hard, wailing cry. I could barely make out what I was writing through the tears, but I did not stop. It actually felt so good to bring all of this emotion to the surface! It was so healing to purge those feelings. The anger that was directed toward her had never been explored before – I didn't even know that it was buried. After writing pages of letting out my inner "you know what," I was exhausted.

Reliving it again during my coaching call with Brenda, I was so happy it happened, because again, I didn't know it was locked deep down inside me and it felt so good to get it out. How could I be mad at my mom though? My sweet, loving, generous, beautiful, kind mother! She didn't do anything to me. She didn't deserve the wrath or words I just delivered - or did she? She was always there for me, right? No. She wasn't. She died. She left me. She wasn't always open with me about what was going on. She didn't share with me the reality of each surgery or treatment. She barely explained what the doctors told her. It was always just "time to fight."

Even at the end, I knew we were getting close because I could see it in her eyes, but it all kind of came out of nowhere. She never sat me down to tell me what was going on. The only time she did, she was in her bedroom with my grandma. When I walked in, she took a deep breath and looked down. She asked my grandma to leave the room. She had me sit close to her and she said, "honey, I'm done fighting."

I always supported her and wanted her to do what was best for her, not for dad or us kids. I hated to see her fight; to lose her hair several times; to go through months of a bone marrow transplant; To deal with experimental medicine and their side effects; not to mention having her breast removed. It was so tough watching her whole life revolve around going to the doctors and checking in and out of hospitals - all to fight cancer. It was awful. I would have supported her decision to stop years prior. She didn't tell me how I could be there for her either. She never wanted to be a burden, but asking for support isn't considered a burden! She never asked for help. Again, how could she leave me? I wasn't ready!

I know that she never meant to hurt me. I know she didn't purposely get cancer. I know she didn't want to die. I know she wanted to be there to watch me and my brother grow up and have families. I know she didn't "do" anything, but the pain didn't know that. The pain somehow crept deep down in the darkest place of my soul and stayed there for a very long time, thus harboring feelings against her. No wonder I had anger issues. No wonder I had short-lived relationships. No wonder I escaped from reality more often than usual. I had this pain aching inside me for so long.

Oh, how that exercise changed my life! I'm so thankful that Brenda gave me that as homework! I finally saw things in a new light and really began to forgive and to heal. I really started to see my life, and hers, with a new perspective. I also got a sense of mom looking at me while I was saying everything to her. She looked apologetic. She understood where I was coming from. It was like she was saying in some way, "you're right honey, I am sorry." I don't need to be right or gain an apology, but that was the look. It was endearing, and it touched my soul. I felt that I really did get some sadness off my heart, and she gladly accepted it as I threw it in her direction. Let's see what comes out for you.

DIG DEEPER #9:
FACE –TO- FACE WITH MOM
Instead of writing another letter, I want you to confront mom by sitting with her and telling her face-to-face.

Choose a place that reminds you of her. If that's too public, sit somewhere you won't be interrupted and envision you are really there. Have with you your favorite picture of her and something important that she gave you that you cherish. This can be a piece of jewelry, a letter, etc.

Sit in a comfortable position. Close your eyes and breathe deeply until you are totally relaxed, and the troubles and thoughts of the day have disappeared.

Picture that you and mom are together at the place that reminds you of her. Maybe you're sitting together at her favorite restaurant or sitting at the dining room table. A place that reminds me of mom is a tea room, but I certainly would not want to have this conversation in a public tea room. Maybe you choose to talk to her on a porch while sitting in rocking chairs, or maybe you're taking a walk together on the beach. Really picture just the two of you together. What do you see? Are there birds chirping?

_____

_____

If there's anyone else around, remove those images. What is she wearing? What are you wearing? Create the scene. This is your moment to embrace her again. Before you begin talking, make sure you can clearly see everything around you and that you feel secure. You may need to do this a few times before you begin talking – that is totally okay! I recommend not talking until you truly see her. She could be any age you want. It can be her before she got sick, or old. This is the healthiest mom you know. She is ready to listen. She is ready to hear your words. She wants you to talk to her and not let anything go unsaid. She has been waiting for you and she is prepared for this moment. She has been waiting for this moment!

If you hear her respond to you – that's great. It's wonderful, but this is for you to open up and to be honest with her about everything you felt, everything you regret, everything you wish she would have done, and everything you're thankful for...I bet you won't need much direction for this "dig deeper." I pray that your words will flow. I hope your tears will be shed. Remember to bring tissues with you. Tons and tons of tissues! Hold the picture of her and the important item tightly. She is with you. She is listening. She loves you and she wants you to heal!

Insight 10:
Gratitude Shift

Simple Abundance: A Daybook of Comfort and Joy by Sarah Ban Breathnach, has been in my bathroom since 1997. Its contents provide a daily motivational thought to ponder. I love this book so much. Highly recommend adding it to your bathroom reading material. On February 26th it read, "The thirteenth-century German philosopher Meister Eckhart, whose teachings so influenced the Quaker movement, believed that "if the only prayer you say in your life is 'thank you,' that would be enough." Are you living a life of gratitude?"

One of my amazing mentors taught me the power of being appreciative; and I will be forever grateful that I was able to attract her into my life because I learned so much from her teachings and by adjusting thought to thanks. Little did I know, that by writing five things I'm grateful for every day, I would produce a life of so much more than I could have ever imagined! Mena, I am forever grateful for your guidance, thought provoking experiences, and supportive love!

If you're not living a life of thanks, it's time for a gratitude shift - because it works! Being thankful attracts abundance. If you haven't caught on to the gratitude game, I strongly encourage you to do so because, as a motherless daughter, we need all the extra love and light this world has to offer us, don't we? Yes, yes, we do!

If you're like me, you probably struggle with bouts of depression. It's not easy to transition from periods when I am happy and thankful to times when I feel alone, sad and non-functional. I get through them by giving thanks for what I have, appreciation for who I am, and gratitude for who I evolved from. And when I'm experiencing my lows, I feel that being thankful helps to remind me that everything is, will be, and always was perfect the way it is meant to be.

Even though I have a major void in my life by not having mom around anymore, I am thankful for the times when I did. When I was going through hard teenage years, she made me feel loved and always believed in me - even though, at times, I made her life a living nightmare. When I was horrific to her at some of her lowest moments, she forgave me. I am thankful that I had her as my mom. And I am grateful that she was a forgiving woman!

Even though we suffer from pain, there is so much to be grateful for. What are you thankful for that mom gave you?

_____

_____

_____

_____

Mine gave me unconditional love, showered me with kind words, encouraged me, and kept a roof over my head and clothes on my back. Looking back at my childhood, I am so thankful that my parents paid for me to participate in sports and made sure I had a birthday party every year. As a kid, I had no concept of how much money they spent on me or how hard my father had to work to provide for us and how mom stretched every penny. They always made sure we had what we needed and, oftentimes, what we wanted. I'm thankful that during the years before I could drive, mom was my chauffeur. She drove me here, there, and everywhere. I never considered how much time of her life she sacrificed for me. I am very grateful. Start to remember the simplest of things that mom gave you, starting with the moment she gave you life. Even if you didn't have the best relationship with her, I'm sure you can find tons of things to be thankful for.

May I also suggest you write down five things every day that you are thankful for? This really shouldn't be too challenging; however, remembering to do it every day may be. Write on beautiful paper, "I am thankful for..." and put it on your makeup mirror or refrigerator - somewhere you can see it every single day. Some days, when I forget to write, I always remember as I am going to sleep.

I give thanks out loud for the beautiful life I have, the amazing people I call family, and my ability to be alive and learn more and more lessons each day. I am thankful for being healthy and grateful for having a bed to sleep in. I thank my car almost daily for being so darn pretty and for running so well. I am grateful that I have a roof over my head and I appreciate the beautiful view it provides. Giving thanks for the smallest of things can produce some big results. When we practice a life of gratitude, we are given more things to be thankful for. I have been practicing gratitude since I was 26 years old and I can confirm that it works!

As I was browsing through my coaching notes when I created the outline to this book, I came across an email from years ago from one of my mentors, Brenda. As she was writing to me regarding my homework, an email came through to her that she thought warranted sharing with me. She wrote, "Also, serendipitously, this came across my email yesterday and I wanted to share this as it is great insight:

Did you know that there is an effective and ineffective way to express gratitude?

Unfortunately, the ineffective way is far more common. It is sort of the default form of gratitude that most people fall into. I was stuck here for a really long time until I found a far more powerful way to practice gratitude, one that moved me into perfect alignment with abundance and greatly accelerated The Law of Attraction.

First, let me talk about the ineffective way to express gratitude. This is gratitude that you express that is related to what is happening in your life right now.

It is closely related to the gratitude and appreciation we learn to express as children (i.e. to say thanks) and that is probably why it is often the default and why so many people get stuck here.

Ineffective gratitude include includes things such as:
- *your health*
- *your relationships*
- *your material possessions*
- *your friends and family*
- *a nice vacation*

I am not saying that there is anything wrong with this form of gratitude. All I'm saying is that it's not nearly as powerful as what I am about to show you.

Often, the problem with the above form of gratitude is that it comes from a place of lack. If you have ever expressed gratitude while thinking, "at least ... I am healthy, or at least I have a great family," then you know what I mean.

This form of gratitude is extremely weak because it is based on the present circumstances. In other words, this form of gratitude is conditional. It makes it sound that you are grateful "only if you have good health, a great relationship, etc."

Unfortunately, conditional gratitude fails to activate the Law of Attraction. The universe is not responding to conditional requests.

The second form of gratitude is complete in that it is a celebration of life itself, for all the experiences you were having. One other key difference is effective gratitude comes from an underlying attitude versus a temporary focus on one item or thing to be grateful for.

With practice, this holistic form of gratitude can become second nature. When it does, the law of attraction will flow far more easily into your life.

The more powerful form of gratitude includes items such as:
- your life
- this awesome planet
- for being who you are for future events; for problems, challenges and hardships
- for your mistakes
- for your mind
- for your freedom

In other words, you become grateful for this amazing journey of your life regardless of what happens and where it takes you because you know that it is right for you and that everything is happening for a reason.

<u>When you're expressing effective gratitude, fear and loss disappear; there is no focus on any lack - and when you reach that state, that is when abundance can really start flowing into your life.</u>

Being grateful for what you have in your life (your health, relationships, etc.) has its place. But when you start feeling truly grateful for everything that is happening in your life and open your heart, you will be amazed at how quickly the universe will start to answer.

So, start creating these feelings now, even in the most unlikely or unpleasant circumstances. And notice how you begin to attract whatever you focus on into your life.

So effective thankfulness can be a practice of being thankful for things that you don't quite have yet. For example, I am thankful for being a millionaire! I am thankful for turning 95! I am thankful for having a six pack! The more I express gratitude for the things I want, I believe, and have seen, the more those things manifest in my life.

When mom died, I had no idea that one day I would own multiple businesses, employ others, start a food truck, or travel to Antarctica - but I have! Even though I have lived through her death and the terrible loss that ensued afterward, I still live a pretty amazing life and I am very thankful for it every single day.

I am also very thankful that I finally was able to publish a book. I have written all my life – I have started many books, but never finished one. I finally decided to write about my story so that I could heal even more and grow from the teachings that came from the words on this paper. I am very blessed and forever grateful!

DIG DEEPER # 10:

Write 10 things you're thankful that mom gave you below. Some suggestions are: family heirlooms, jewelry, her favorite sweatshirt; or they can be things like time, rides to the movies, back-to-school clothes every year. Go back to your earliest memory and see what comes up.

1. _____

2. _____

3. _____

4. _____

5. _____

6. _____

7. _____

8. _____

9. _____

10. _____

Insight 11:
Keeping Mom Alive

I began doing these "dig deepers" over ten years ago through my coaching and personal development. Assembling my thoughts and strategies, and publishing them in the form of this book, has been an insightful process. What's more, is that I'm now able to share them with you. I had to choose the information and the "dig deepers" that impacted me the most on my journey; and I also had to decide how to make the insights and experiences flow to best support forgiveness and healing. As I was re-reading my own homework from the past, I carefully chose these eleven insights I'm sharing with you. I chose to focus on eleven because I think of mom whenever I see 1:11 or 11:11. Whether it's the time on the clock or the change received after paying a tab, I see number ones every day, everywhere.

If you look up angel numbers online, you will find that the number one resonates with new beginnings, independence, creativity, and self-development. Supposedly, it appears to remind you that you create your own reality, intentions and actions. Isn't that a nice reminder? That's also why I priced this book at $11.11. Additionally, I purposefully finished writing the manuscript to this book on February 11th. Do you have special numbers that pop up in your world? What do you think they mean? What do you think about when they do? Seek out their "meanings" and see if it jives with your thoughts.

I feel extremely blessed to be able to write and share my experiences with others; it's something I have always wanted to do. Little did I know that by working on self-development for all those years, I was actually self-motivating myself into writing my first published piece! This is very powerful for me and I hope that it has been powerful for you. Congratulations, you are on the last insight!

Here are a few questions to ponder based on what you've read so far:

Have you restored forgotten memories?

_____

_____

What has come to the surface that has lightened your emotional load?

_____

_____

_____

_____

Have you embraced forgiveness?

_____

_____

Have you experienced a sense of healing? If so,
how?

_____

_____

_____

_____

To heal is to become healthy again. Are you
living a healthier life than when you first began
this process? If yes, please describe how:

_____

_____

_____

_____

If not, do you feel as if there is anything blocking
you from achieving healing? Are you fighting
yourself? Do your best to go inward. It took me
18 years to get to a place I truly believe is

healthy, so this doesn't happen overnight, unfortunately. The death of mom is serious trauma, no matter how close you were with her.

_____

_____

Whether you took a year to get here, or if you sped through the insights over a weekend, there should definitely be a shift in your thoughts and feelings associated with mom's death and your life since. From dealing with the day she died to confronting her face-to-face, you have definitely dug deep. I pray this has helped your ability to live a healthier, more loving life. If it hasn't... read it again at another time and see if there is a better result.

So, what's next? How do you keep living a life of forgiveness that's filled with continued healing? Notice your reactions and NON-reactions to moments that bring up emotions of pain or happiness. Again, notice the universe's nudge! In order to further your healing, talk to people openly about your experiences and keep those dialogues going. Keep journaling as well. There is no cure for the aftermath of mom's death, but there are ways to make it less painful as you navigate the rest of your life. Keep mom alive and watch what continues to change.

Include mom in your world. Invite her into your daily life!

What were her favorite kinds of flowers?
Make it a priority to have those fresh flowers in the house more often. You can even plant them in a pot in your backyard. If they're seasonal, set a reminder on your phone to go to the market to grab seeds, a beautiful pot, fertilizer and a cute watering can. Make this an annual tradition that you look forward to.

Pass her jewelry along.
Those pieces that you don't want to get rid of, but never wear, could be perfect for a friend. Tell them how important the piece is and how you want them to love it the way mom did. They will keep her spirit alive by telling others where the piece came from. Possessing jewelry that is worn infrequently doesn't seem right. I recently gave a beautiful sea salt pink pearl necklace to a girlfriend who was wearing a shirt that I knew it would complement. I never wore the strands that I acquired after mom passed. Seeing them radiate on my friend's neck was special.

Use the good china and crystal!
Mom decided well before she passed that it was silly to own china that was used only a few times a year. Therefore, she got rid of the cheap plates and bowls and replaced them with her wedding china. She disposed of the heavy box that hid the sterling silverware that was only used on Thanksgiving. "It's real silver spoons from now on," she proclaimed one day! I inherited these and use them daily. I actually forgot that they were real until I wrote this. It's good to know in case times get tough! Just kidding!

Look at pictures and videos more often.
Don't wait for her anniversary. Don't only pull them out when you're missing her. Watch them and look at them when you're having a great day. Share these pleasant moments with her during happy times! If you have loved ones who may not have seen them, invite them over and go down memory lane together. If there are others in the videos or pictures - make copies and send them along with a hand-written card. Tell them, if you know, what they meant to mom. You will make their month!

Hang a memorial wall.

At first, I had pictures of mom all over my place, but then they made me sad, so I took them all down. As I said before, I have begun putting them up again. If you don't like displaying pictures all around the house, find a place where you can hang multiple pictures, maybe in a single grouping, in one area. Your closet, the laundry room, or somewhere less visible might work better for you. I love it again. I'll walk past a picture of mom and say, "hi mom."

Talk to her.

This is really powerful; however, it was strange for me at first, but then it really helped me. Mom has been with me as I've written this book. She has guided me. She even helped me find lost pages of coaching calls that I needed to complete a thought. She has been listening, and boy have I been talking. I find it very therapeutic to talk to her openly now. I speak out loud and I don't wait to hear anything back, but just talking to mom makes me feel better inside. I thank her all the time. I also think that she helps me get the parking spaces in the front. I play a game where I say. "give me VIP parking" and nine out of ten times, I get it. Then I say, "thanks, mom!"

Write to her.
This may become more intimate than talking. I find that when I write with a pen or on the keyboard, words take on a life of their own. Something in my brain clicks when I write. Buried thoughts arise and often, questions are answered. Writing is very different than talking. I highly recommend it. Write on! (I got that from my editor, Sean.)

Talk about her more to friends.
Lately, I have been pleasantly surprised to have had a positive response while talking about mom with friends. I feel supported and heard. It has also opened the conversation up to allow them to talk about some of their painful experiences and happy memories. It has created deeper bonds with loved ones.

Read her letters.
I do this often. No longer do I wait for those special days to read her letters. Every time I do, I find some kind of hidden message that was meant for me at that very moment. This has become very special to me. Each time they are new all over again. If you have letters, put them in a beautiful box and display them.

Buy her favorite perfume.

Mom didn't wear perfume, so I cannot relate to this one. My dear friend Joey, who lost his mom when he was five, found the perfume his mom wore. He bought it and he sprays it when he wants to recall memories from those early days when he was young, and she was still alive. If mom had worn perfume, I certainly would be spraying it often! I would even keep it in one of those gorgeous perfume spray bottles.

Make her favorite cookies on her birthday or yours!

For my birthday last year, I made snickerdoodles – that's all I wanted to do! Mom and I used to make them together all the time when I was young. It was a way that I was able to have her with me on my birthday. After all, it's the day that she gave me life!

Are there places you know she wanted to go? Visit them and take her soul with you. Before mom died, my father took her to many places that she wanted to go. I don't recall any places that she truly wanted to visit before she died that she didn't get to go to; however, not everyone has the time to plan out their last days - or the resources to execute the plan. If you know a place where mom would have wanted to go – then GO! And take something of hers with you; whether it's wearing a piece of jewelry she left behind or taking a picture of her and putting it in your wallet.

DIG DEEPER #11:
To honor mom, I recommend that you continue to heal. Take action in your life. Be the woman (or man) that she would be proud of. Make changes. Be accountable for where you are right now, and then decide where you want to go. You have the power within you - and you have her by your side. Whether she supported you in life or not, she supports you in her death. Believe that, have faith in that.

Help others. Share your story with them and help them heal. Teach them to forgive as you have. Maybe even start a support group where friends who have lost their moms can come together, share their journeys, and talk freely with other women who understand their challenges and pain on a different level. I plan on doing this next, because I strongly believe that this is a story that will continue. As I grow and evolve, more will emerge and manifest in my life - and mom still won't be there.

Continuing to heal will forever be a part of my life and having a solid support system around me is definitely desired.

Visit this book annually and see if your answers change or expand. Create your own "dig deepers." Ask yourself hard questions and get to the root of your pain. Invite others to do the same. Share this book with them and be there to support them. Recommend this book to moms who are dying, or daughters who are in the process of losing their moms. This book is even great for any mom; because you simply never know. Doing these "dig deepers" can protect others from future pain associated with death.

Thank you for going on this journey with me. Thank you for your strength and desire to forgive and heal. I applaud you for your courage and willingness to dig deeper. Life may never be the same without mom, but creating a world in which she exists, is still possible.

Lots of love to you!

Mom as a young lady.

My brother and me in St. Martin just days after learning of
Mom's first cancer diagnosis - August 1990.

We are at my Army basic training graduation at Fort Jackson, South Carolina - May 1999.

This was taken on a beautiful Saturday in St. Petersburg, Florida during the first ever "Making Strides Against Breast Cancer Walk" to support the American Cancer Society. Mom and I made the front page in the *St. Petersburg Times*. She originally did not want to go, but woke up that morning and asked me to get her a wheelchair so she could participate on my team. This is how I became connected with the American Cancer Society. After volunteering for this walk, they asked me to come in to interview for a position - October 1999.

This was Mom's last Thanksgiving. I asked her to teach me
how to make a turkey. I didn't want to get up early, but
she yelled at me (which she never did) and said, "if you
want to do this, this is the time to do it." I believe she knew
it was going to be her last Thanksgiving. I did not know -
November 1999.

This is where Mom spent most of her last days. Blackie
our beloved cat was always right next to her –
January 2000.

This was taken at my Mom's last dinner. She wanted to go to Salt Rock Grill in Indian Rocks, Florida. It was very emotional - January 2000.

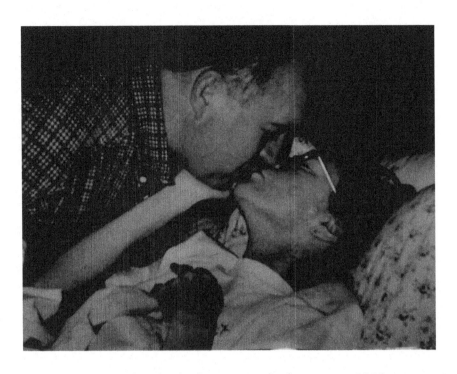

This was taken the day before mom died - January 2000.

Acknowledgements

It isn't easy writing a book about your life, in which you share experiences with strangers; in fact, it is a little scary. I am very proud of myself for sticking to my desires and holding myself accountable. I am thankful for everyone who encouraged me along this long journey.

Family:
Dad, I thank you for allowing me to ask you questions about the past, even though I am sure they were painful to revisit. I also thank you for understanding that I needed to tell my perspective in order to truly heal.

Thank you, Rae Ann, for always being there to listen. Even though you're more like a sister, you have shown me mother qualities that are very appreciated.

Jean, you were the first one there for me after mom died and I have always admired you and thought of you as a mother figure. I miss you and your weekend visits.

Loves:

Chris, I am so thankful for your ears. I feel so bad for you sometimes, having to listen to me. I am grateful. You have always been the best shoulder to cry on. You know when I'm affected from a TV show or when I have a memory pop up. Your attentive nature and loving eyes have been such a blessing to me and I am very grateful that you're in my world!

Joey, you're my angel! I love that you're my best friend and my spiritual guide. We have so much fun together and we share the bond of not having our moms. Thank you for always being there for me and always being my biggest fan - and for your unconditional loyalty.

Tarra, I miss you and I absolutely hate that you had to lose your mom. I always felt we were brought together because I was able to give you a glimpse of your future reality. I love you very much and I pray for peace for you.

Mentors:

Cheri was my first professional mentor and I admired her so much. She sat on the board at the American Cancer Society and was my volunteer partner on the area's Cattle Baron's

Ball. She demonstrated poise, confidence and strength. She also lost her mom and knew that as young as I was, how hard it must have been for me. She believed in me. She taught me so much and I miss her friendship tremendously since I moved away.

Mena, I really cannot thank you enough. I have grown more since you were my coach and I have realized just how much you helped me see things differently. I am so honored that you saw something in me when you invested your time in helping shape my world. I am forever grateful.

Miss Brenda, I love how we met and I cherish our friendship story. Thank you for letting me encourage you to begin coaching me. What a trip! You were, and are, a natural and I feel very blessed that we had the time to grow together. Who knows what the future holds...

Thank you to my dear Mom. You have been the best co-author along this journey. I am forever grateful that I had the time with you that I did and that I know I chose you to be my mother. I miss you. I miss you so much! Know that I am determined to live a love-filled life and will do my best to be a woman that you would be proud of!

AND, I am very thankful for YOU!

About the Author

I was born and raised in Pennsylvania and lived there until I was twelve. We moved when my father got a job in beautiful Pinellas County, Florida. We really lucked out as he could have gone anywhere in the states being in the economic development field. Moving in the seventh grade was challenging, but I feel very blessed to have ended up in the sunshine state.

I got my start in non-profit management in 1998 when I volunteered for the American Cancer Society's Making Strides Against Breast Cancer event. I discovered the walk at mom's house when I went to throw something away. There was a MSABC postcard sitting on top of the trash can. I grabbed it. It was the first ever event in the Tampa Bay area and I wanted to help. I asked mom if she wanted to do it with me and she said firmly, "no!" I went to work the next day at The Men's Wearhouse and called the corporate office to find out what I was allowed to do in our store and they explained that they would match dollar for dollar every cent I raised and that I could hang up posters, distribute buttons, and basically do anything to promote the cause. I was tickled. I called the area MSABC headquarters and told them my story. I told them how mom had fought cancer for the past ten years and was diagnosed when I was only ten years old. I told them where I worked and that I wanted to help. I didn't think anything of it, but you would have thought that the woman on the other end of the phone thought she hit the jackpot! I hadn't even told her I was going to get dollar for dollar matching funds from my employer.

I didn't realize how unique my situation was. She asked if she could deliver a team packet to me that day and I said, "of course." She was a petite thing and she asked me to be a media volunteer. Of course, I said I would do whatever they needed. I had to go to training at their office and, during the meeting, I asked the woman training us if she was also a volunteer. She explained that this is what she did for a living. I knew at that moment that I had found my calling. I couldn't believe that I could get paid to fight cancer. Sign me up!

Our team raised $2,000 - and two and a half months later, I got a phone call to come in to interview for an administrative position. As you read, the first day on the job was the day of mom's viewing. I took on more and more responsibilities and finally got promoted (to the position that my trainer had) after a year and a half.

With the support of countless volunteers, I was able to raise millions of dollars for different charities around the world - all because that job catapulted me into the nonprofit sector. I worked my way up to Development Director and then left to start my own fundraising business in San Diego. I ended up in California after coming home from a deployment in Kuwait during Operation Enduring & Iraq Freedom. I joined the Army Reserves in 1998 to help pay for my college education.

After leaving the non-profit sector in 2007, I started Buy Me Love Benefits, an event production company where singles met and made a difference. I basically got amazing single men and women to choose a charity, create a date package, and then I auctioned them off. It was such a fun gig to start in my late twenties. I met amazing people and raised thousands of dollars by hosting these exciting parties!

I moved to Daytona Beach in 2008 to be close to my father after he underwent a bypass surgery. It was there that I created Callan Group Communications, a boutique communications agency focused on public relations, digital marketing, association management and business development. I was awarded one of "The Most Influential Women in Business" by The Volusia/Flagler Business Report in 2012 and 2014 and I have been honored to sit on numerous charitable boards.

My most recent endeavor was purchasing a food truck. I kept the delicious food on wheels operation going for three years. During that time, I created and still have the Food Truck Movement - in which we do marketing for food trucks, scheduling and support owners with catering options.

As you can see, I love to work, but I do play quite a bit too. Since my business gives me the freedom to work remotely, I travel a lot! I've been to Australia, Antarctica, Norway, France, Ireland, Germany, Greece, Italy, The Netherlands, Turkey, Israel, Kuwait, all over North America, Argentina, Chile, Uruguay and Canada. I recently dove (pun intended) into snorkeling and I get to visit the Caribbean often! I have a longtime boyfriend named Chris who has been my rock for years. I also still live close to my dad and have been blessed to have a special relationship with him.

And I am now a published author! Thank you! Thank you very much!

I am only thirty-eight, so I have many more years to live and so much more to learn!

Let's Connect!
To learn more about the "After Mom" coaching program, how to start a community support group or for speaking requests, please email –
UniverseNudge@gmail.com
Facebook – www.Facebook.com/UniverseNudge
Instagram – www.Instagram.com/UniverseNudge

Made in the USA
Monee, IL
27 April 2020

27963715R10089